# JOHN WESLEY
# A Pictorial Journey

## by
# JOHN HURST

This book is a tribute to World Methodism and in particular, the people of the new Millennium who strive to keep alive the work of John Wesley. It is through their passion for ministry and service, often in difficult circumstances, that we can all gain spiritual strength, thus providing a greater sense of purpose in our lives.

Picture credits   All reproductions of watercolours and narrative by John Hurst.

Journal quotes of John Wesley in italics.

Photographs by G. L. Trinder.
Foreword by Nigel Collinson.

Published by   John Hurst Fine Arts © 2003.
Epworth, North Lincolnshire, England.

The moral right of the author has been asserted.

Type setting and editing, Jacqui Hurst.

Consultant, Max Gray.

Printed in England by RCS.

ISBN No 0-9544400-1-3

THE MARKET CROSS, EPWORTH

# Contents

| | |
|---|---|
| Foreword by N. Collinson | 9 |
| From Within the Parsonage-A Starting Place | 10 |
| Robin Hood's Bay, North East Yorkshire | 12 |
| The Great Elm of Bag Enderby, Lincolnshire | 14 |
| Brakenbury's Bequest, Raithby | 16 |
| Gloster House, Co. Offaly, Ireland | 18 |
| A Field by the Ruin, Adare | 20 |
| The Kingdom of the Palatines, Ballingrane | 22 |
| To the City, London | 24 |
| The Warm Rooms, Wesley's House | 26 |
| Langham Row-A Marshland Place, Lincolnshire | 28 |
| Newbiggin, The Oldest of the Old, Yorkshire | 30 |
| The Eight Walls of Yarm | 32 |
| Wednesbury. A Mob-Like the Roaring of the Sea | 34 |
| Bristol, Staging Post for the South West | 36 |
| Carn Brea. The View from Above | 38 |
| Gwennap. The Tin Miners' Legacy | 40 |
| The Heppingstock of St. Buryan | 42 |
| A Tale of Ursula Triggs | 44 |
| Jack's House, Trewint | 46 |
| Bexley. A Journey to the South East | 48 |
| Shoreham. Into the Darent Valley | 50 |
| Garth. The Romance and the Robin | 52 |
| 'The Star' below Devauden Hill | 54 |
| Newcastle, Third Point of the Triangle | 56 |
| Methodists in Calderdale | 58 |
| Mount Zion. Yorkshire Grit | 60 |
| The Manors of Oxfordshire | 62 |
| Oxford. Methodical Living | 64 |
| Edinburgh. Over the Firths to the Totum Kirkie | 66 |
| Banff. Charm by the Edge of the Sea | 68 |
| Epworth. Home at Last | 70 |

## Colour Plates

| | |
|---|---|
| John Wesley, J. M. Williams | 2 |
| The Market Place, Epworth | 3 |
| The Artist's Journey | 8 |
| Epworth Old Rectory | 11 |
| A View into the Bay | 13 |
| Mystical Monolith | 15 |
| Raithby, The Courtyard Chapel | 17 |
| The Saloon Gallery, Gloster House | 19 |
| The Franciscan Abbey, Adare | 21 |
| Ballingrane Chapel | 23 |
| Wesley's House, City Road, London | 25 |
| John Wesley's Study | 27 |
| Fenland Reed, Langham Row | 29 |
| Newbiggin, from Fellowship Farm | 31 |
| Yarm Octagonal Chapel | 33 |
| Francis Asbury's House | 35 |
| Interior, New Room, Bristol | 37 |
| Carn Brea, A Vantage Point | 39 |
| Gwennap Pit | 41 |
| The Squire's Mounting Block | 43 |
| Angrouse, Mullion | 45 |
| Trewint Cottage | 47 |
| St. Mary's Church, Bexley | 49 |
| The Old Vicarage, Shoreham | 51 |
| The Wedding Route, Garth | 52 |
| Landscape, The Black Mountains | 55 |
| The Keelman's Hospital, Newcastle | 57 |
| Heptonstall, Chapel on the Terrace | 59 |
| Mount Zion, Bradfield | 61 |
| Finstock Manor | 63 |
| Lincoln College, Oxford | 65 |
| Bailie Fyfe's Close. Edinburgh | 67 |
| Old Fife Street, Banff | 69 |
| Epworth Old Rectory | 71 |
| Joyce Pooley and the Artist | 80 |

## Tonal Drawings

| | |
|---|---|
| These Epworth Lawns | 6 |
| Samuel Wesley's Grave | 10 |
| Whitby Abbey | 12 |
| The Lincolnshire Wolds | 14 |
| Raithby Chapel Interior | 16 |
| The Irish Demesne | 18 |
| Derelict Farmstead, C. Clare | 20 |
| A Horn to make the Valleys Ring | 22 |
| The Powerhouse of Methodism | 24 |
| The Chancel, St. Paul's Cathedral | 26 |
| Wesley's Pulpit, Newbiggin | 30 |
| Tin Mine, Redruth | 38 |
| The Gatepost Pulpit, Gwennap | 40 |
| St. Michael's Mount | 42 |
| The Hearth, Wesley's Cottage | 46 |
| The Old Yew, Shoreham | 48 |
| River Wye, Builth Wells | 53 |
| The Road to the West | 54 |
| Arbroath Totum Kirkie | 66 |
| The Rectory Croft | 70 |
| The River Spey | 79 |

THESE EPWORTH LAWNS

# Introduction

Autumn rain is lashing the ancient orchard trees. It is the 24th September 2001 and already the fruits are lying scattered across these Epworth lawns. Despite this outward turmoil, my spirit has been lifted by a recent conversation with a minister from Ireland, a land I have only seen on a tattered road map. The technological wizardry of web pages, route planners, on-line ferry timetables and the mobile telephone, has already created all the forward logistics enabling me to journey across Britain and Ireland in search of John Wesley's inimitable places. The telephone conversation I have just had with the Reverend Ivor Owens has filled me with apprehension and anticipation of the spiritual journey about to be undertaken. He offered to meet me in Tullamore, Co. Offaly to show me the interesting saloon at Gloster House, on the road from Birr to Roscrea. We know from his journals that Wesley was marooned in Holyhead on April 12th 1749 while waiting for his ship. Our vessel, the Dublin Swift sails at 09.15 on the 22nd October and takes under two hours to skim the waves.

So let the journey begin. By air, boat, train, car or foot I will seek obscure and interesting places where Mr Wesley preached and lifted the hearts of those around him.

John Hurst, Epworth 2001

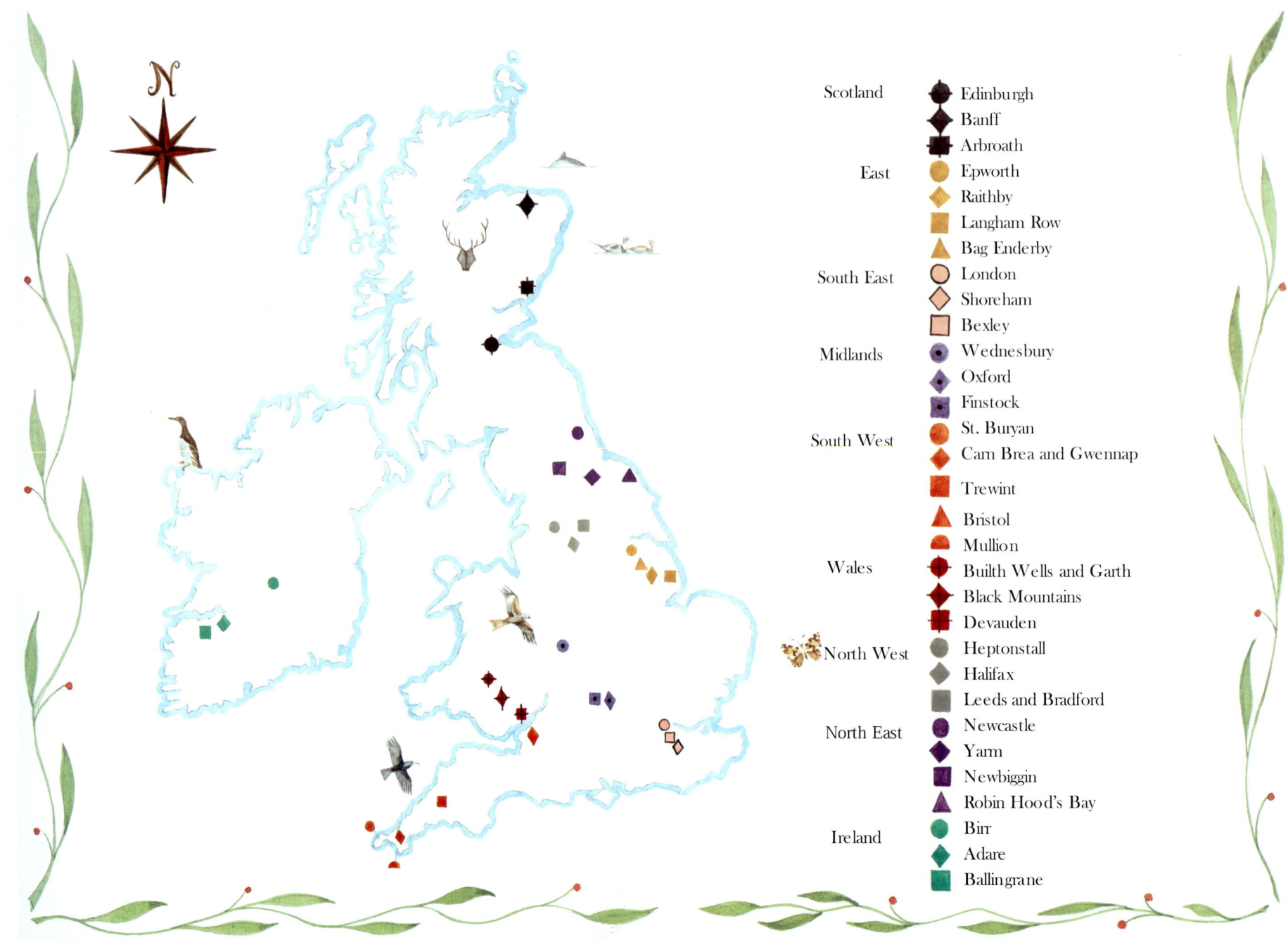

8 THE ARTIST'S JOURNEY

# Foreword

## John Wesley
## A Pictorial Journey

Most days I glance into the large hall in Methodist Church House in London's Marylebone Road. There, together with the rolls on which are listed the names of former missionaries which so inspired Dietrich Bonhoeffer when he first saw them in Richmond College, is hung the dramatic picture of the fire at the Old Rectory. It depicts the young Wesley being rescued by an Epworth villager who is standing on the shoulders of a companion. Thoughtfully, he has taken off his shoes, which now lie to one side amid pots and pans and buckets of water.

As I read *A Pictorial Journey,* I fancy John Hurst has put on those shoes and taken us on a journey that links the brand plucked from the burning with his twenty-first century heirs and joins the Lincolnshire village of Epworth with buildings and landscapes throughout Britain and Ireland. It is a remarkable journey and a beautiful book, full of colour and detail, the sound of rivers and the calling of birds. John Hurst's keen eye and ear remind us that the eighteenth century world was, on the whole, a quieter place. Whether walking, riding horseback or in his carriage, John Wesley might well have been just as aware of his surroundings.

As we turn these pages in this tercentenary year of John Wesley's birth, perhaps we may be led to ask how we should celebrate his legacy now in a world vastly changed. Wesley would have embraced that change, for he and Charles pictured it also in the inward life of growing holiness in which a person is *changed from glory into glory.* So, amidst these old stones, there is always the possibility of new thoughts of God, fresh stirrings of faith and larger horizons of the human spirit.

Nigel Collinson
Secretary of the Methodist Conference

# From Within the Parsonage - A Starting Place

For me, no other room in Epworth Old Rectory evokes a feeling of such constant peace and pure calm as the one known today as The Period Room. Originally Susanna and Samuel Wesley's bedchamber, it is situated on the south-west corner of the house and enjoys the full glory of afternoon sunlight. It is here that Susanna would retire at 5 pm for her constitutional meditation, reading and writing. I decided to spend my meditational time composing colour notes and line drawings here, before starting on my pilgrimage. The light, so conducive to this space, came flooding in and I became conscious of the frailty and unique beauty of a patchwork quilt that lay before my eyes. Made by the Bolton sisters of Witney and Finstock in Oxfordshire around 1780, it was used by John Wesley on many occasions and finally found its way to his family home some years ago. It is at this point that I remembered my time in the building as a five year old. Although feeling guilty that my parents were unaware of my daily clambering among the crumbling brickwork of a partially restored rectory, I could still recollect the place leaving me with a feeling of awe and especially, well-being.

Looking west, one may gaze upon the fine Rectory gardens. A woodland path meanders by shrubberies to a herbaceous border, while holly and yew form a timeless amphitheatre beneath the spreading boughs of a magnificent beech. When considering the special artefacts in the room one cannot ignore the rocking cradle and recall Susanna's desire for children to 'cry quietly and fear the rod'. A large bible chair stands in the corner with a clever dual-purpose design enabling the owner the kneel before an open bible placed upon a concealed pivoting shelf. The bed itself had a roped mattress, the ropes pulled taut for greater comfort and giving rise to the old saying 'sleep tight'. As the blinds were drawn, returning the room to its subdued museum conditions, I became aware that in 1735 Samuel died here and on speaking to his daughter Emily, said "Do not be concerned at my death; God will then begin to manifest himself to my family." As I stood in silence beneath the great ship's timber, a distant light glowed from another place and again the enduring feeling of constant peace cocooned me. Strengthened by this I then proceeded on my travels in search of further hallowed realms. Although not wanting to leave, I did so knowing my faith had been reaffirmed by the simple truth and belief in that which is good.

SAMUEL WESLEY'S GRAVE

EPWORTH OLD RECTORY INTERIOR

# Robin Hood's Bay

We returned to Epworth at 8 pm, passing harvesters that were clearing the fields before a threatening storm. Our journey, accompanied by great humidity and sticky heat, had taken us from the shimmering high moors of North Yorkshire, splendid in their new haze of purple heather, down to the Vale of York with its pastoral elegance.

Robin Hood's Bay remains intact as a fine example of human resilience, despite a precarious existence on the coast. As I stood on the quay where John Wesley had preached, now washed by an ebbing tide, I could only wonder at his courage when taking The Word to these hardy Yorkshire folk on 24th June 1761. It is here that *"In the midst of the sermon, a large cat, frightened out of a chamber leapt down upon a woman's head and ran over the shoulders of many more; but none of them moved or cried out any more than if it had been a butterfly."* Further testimony to Wesley's respect for their lifestyle was found in the old chapel, now a library and café. A small display states that although preaching in Robin Hood's Bay eleven times, not once did he point an accusing finger at local smuggling, an issue often brought to the fore elsewhere.

Beside a calm and crystal blue summer sea, the image before me was one of true nostalgia. Each remnant of finely crafted brick, door panel and stone, hewn and fitted so deftly in place by the time John Wesley visited, still seemed to exude profound strength. Such is a fitting tribute to those indigenous people who still dwell there to this day.

At that time I knew very little of the people whom John Wesley would seek out for his congregations. From seafaring souls of Yorkshire to the hardened iron workers of Wednesbury, the tin miners of Redruth and the displaced Palatines of Ireland; all of society would be drawn towards the experience of his influential preaching. Yet also, another unknown treat lay ahead, for I was soon to meet the Methodists of The New Millenium, many of whom are guardians of a special place or part of a unique historical heritage. All of them would extend a warm welcome to the weary traveller like their forebears had done to Wesley. This would prove beyond doubt that Methodism is firmly rooted in the society of today, be it in the four corners of our kingdom or the world itself.

WHITBY ABBEY

A VIEW INTO THE BAY

# The Great Elm of Bag Enderby

I travelled to Harrington Hall today in order to present my patrons with two architectural garden studies. A chance conversation with them regarding the preaching locations of John Wesley resulted in a remarkable find. It appears that nestling amidst the rolling Lincolnshire Wolds lies the tiny settlement of Bag Enderby and within its parish on an ancient green stands the remains of a time worn monolith.

This bleached eroded trunk is all that remains of a great elm, under which it is said John Wesley delivered his uplifting words. How mystical its hollows, gnarls and embedded hand made iron nails, a testimony to mans' interaction with it.

As I pondered upon its age and form, enhanced by the change and light of a vast cumulus sky, a quiet sense of timeless peace surged forth from within the Great Elm of Bag Enderby.

MYSTICAL MONOLITH

# Brackenbury's Bequest

On the 6th October 2001, it dawned breezy and cloud laden. I wandered excitedly across the gracious lawns of Sausthorpe Hall within the wolds of Lincolnshire, seeking out those intriguing viewpoints that watercolourists dream about. Colour notes were compiled regarding a quaint apple tree, antique wheelbarrow, sundial and sparkling rill, reflecting the distant stubble and wooded landscape beyond, in its clear pools.

With guarded expectation, thoughts soon drifted towards Raithby, a few miles away. I knew that the chapel there was of special significance, being provided for worship by the generous patronage of Robert Carr Brackenbury in 1779 and actually dedicated by John Wesley on 5th July of that year. Robert Carr Brackenbury was a frequent travelling companion of John Wesley, accompanying him on many occasions, particularly to Holland. With his fine command of the French language he also established good Methodist connections on the island of Jersey. It was noted that on 3rd June 1779, the squire was 'very fatigued' when travelling away from Arbroath and Aberdeen. Was he perhaps in awe of the fact that his own chapel dedication was due to take place in a month of that date? He died in 1818, having solemnly expressed the wish that 'his fame might not be made the subject of human panegyric'.

On arriving in Raithby I could not find the little chapel until tentatively entering into what appeared to be a very private walled courtyard. There in the corner, neatly placed and almost secreted behind a low wall, stood the oldest intact Lincolnshire chapel. Adjacent brick arches of the old estate stables and coach-house, complemented perfectly the matching arched lintels above both entrance doors and the finely glazed sash windows of the chapel. Entering this unique place one may ascend one of two stairways, originally the male and female access. Both are exquisitely designed, the turned balustrades an example of fine eighteenth century craftsmanship repeated elsewhere throughout the building.

Silence reigned in Raithby chapel, now suspended in time with only the swaying boughs of a churchyard sycamore infringing upon that hallowed space. One could sense by contrast the passion of praise and song that would have reverberated from the very structure when John Wesley took part in the dedication service.

**CHAPEL INTERIOR**

RAITHBY, THE COURTYARD CHAPEL

# Gloster House - 21st October 2001

Gloster House stands by the road from Birr to Roscrea, Co. Offaly, Ireland. Standing in its own finely terraced gardens and demesne of ponds, arbours and carefully selected vistas, this once proud structure would have presented the grandest of pulpits from which Mr Wesley could speak. The location of Gloster within Glasderry More, or Big Green Wood, situated in the very centre of Ireland and en route from Dublin to Limerick, would have suited our traveller very well.

Cloaked in autumn drizzle beneath a great avenue of limes, I glimpsed the architectural splendour created by Sir Edward Lovatt Pearce between 1699 and 1733. Described by deBreffny and Ffolliott in 'The Houses of Ireland', as having 'a notable 18th Century façade and elegant interior, combined with a deep arcaded gallery which overlooked the saloon', it soon became apparent that this was to be an exhilarating visit. I was welcomed by Tom Alexander, the new owner who was warming body and soul by a huge roaring fire of rotting timber within the courtyard. Away from the threatening rain, I entered what remains of a grandiose eighteenth century world of lofty chambers, coffered barrel vaulted ceilings and elegant niches. From once polished floors, I craned my neck upwards towards a delicate curved railing, the Gloster House pulpit of Mr John Wesley. It is stated that lesser mortals listened from where I stood, while nobles were placed above and behind our preacher.

After climbing the stairs I reached the very place and sensed an awesome grandeur, almost whispered by the flaking paint and dust strewn boards. The distant vista of blues framed by towering yews, echoed this sentiment of faded elegance. How Wesley must have relished this fine theatre on 13th June 1749, in which to preach his uplifting words to the Irish people. After compiling sketches in the grounds and colour notes of the interior, I left Tom with his spitting embers, contemplating the formidable renovation of Gloster House, his mission being to create once again a residence of notable and elegant proportions.

THE SALOON GALLERY, GLOSTER HOUSE

# A Field by the Ruin

The town of Adare stands upon the road between Limerick and Rathkeale. Adare is derived from 'Ath Dara, the ford of the oak' and is famed for its three abbeys, castle and manor house surrounded by fine golf courses and equestrian paddocks set within the 'Golden Vale' of the Maigue, Camoge and Deel rivers. When Wesley preached here in 1765, the location was described as 'a field beside a Franciscan ruin' near a walled town. Many disagree with the latter as Adare was never walled! However, the friary still stands much as it would have done 236 years ago and since 1976, a simple stone has marked the place where Wesley stood in the shade of an ash tree. This Franciscan ruin stands within the old Dunraven Estate. Built in 1464, it played an integral part alongside the other notable settlements, creating a pattern of river trade along the Maigue and nearby Shannon rivers. The term 'Golden' refers to the wealth of dairy products for which the region is still famed.

It was into this arena that John Wesley stepped. He had already influenced the Palatines and rubbed shoulders with the aristocracy of Gloster House, so here I visualise him speaking to all who would be familiar with the abbey site. How often do we see him choose a significant landmark in order to be clearly heard and seen. As I viewed the ancient stones and lichen matted towers in 2001, a vision came into my mind. The pristine golf greens became rough pasture and people clamoured around those crumbling walls, jostling for a vantage point to hear the preacher.

Although many years have passed, the annual field meeting held by Adare Methodists at the abbey site, now takes place on the first Tuesday during June. The one hundred and eighty fourth meeting was held in 2002. The golf course is always closed on that day to avoid the danger of flying golf balls, such is the lasting empathy and appreciation of John Wesley's impact upon the people of Adare.

DERELICT FARMSTEAD, COUNTY CLARE

THE FRANCISCAN ABBEY, ADARE

# The Kingdom of the Palatines

Travelling south west from Limerick into a rolling landscape of verdant pastures hedged by aged thorns, we came upon the tiny church of Ballingrane.  The writer, Tom Nester, in his book 'The Keeper of Absalom's Island', described being there as 'standing on the perimeter of a different world. Everywhere there was order, trimmed hedges, limed walls and houses as white as driven snow'.  The inhabitants are descendents of the German Palatines who settled in the south-western region between Adare and Rathkeale during 1709, building this little church in 1766 on a site donated by the Heck family.  Barbara Heck (nee Ruttle) along with Philip Embury, emigrated to New York in August 1760, forming the earliest Methodist Society on the north American continent in 1766.  It is stated that Philip Embury preached the first sermon there to five people, four of whom came from Ballingrane.  It is also evident that the conversion of the Palatines occurred as a result of John Wesley's many visits to the region; ten to thirteen in all and although he described them as *"...much given to debauchery"* he also found within them *"...much life"* in a purely religious sense.

Stepping into the simple church I was immediately influenced by the peaceful atmosphere, despite the region's tumultuous history.  It is little wonder that the Palatines converted to Methodism en mass following Embury and Heck across the Atlantic.  My eye was then drawn towards an ancient horn that hung against the north wall, a horn that according to locals, could 'make the valleys ring' summoning folk from their labours.  They came from far and wide to worship, particularly when Mr Wesley was abroad.  We retired to 'Fortview', the family home of the Ruttles, where John Purdy the local minister introduced us to Brian Ruttle.  Here, I was able to view the pear tree grown from the grafted scion of the original tree under which Wesley preached. "Trees are doubtful" stated the Reverend Dudley Cooney in his notes to me from Dublin and I remembered the elm at Bag Enderby, yet on speaking with Brian I was convinced about this tree and accepted the only pear hanging on it, to sow seeds in Epworth.  After thanking our hosts we retraced our steps to Clonunion House, spending our final hours in Ireland, looking towards the mountains, as evening light cast a hue of naples yellow over the peat laden waters of the Shannon.

A HORN TO 'MAKE THE VALLEYS RING'

BALLINGRANE CHAPEL

# To the City

In a lifetime of early rising, John Wesley must have often left Epworth while most of the village slept. On 7th November 2001, as burnished tints of autumn oak began to vaguely light up a dull grey dawn, I also began a journey. I was travelling to another place where John Wesley had lived and preached. My mission was to commit to memory and this book, my vision of his London home.

Wesley's journeys were slow by standards we take for granted today and I was to reflect on this while cocooned against the elements in a high speed train. Never forgetting my faith, I couldn't help contemplating whether God is nearer to a horseback traveller than to a passenger on a train. I covered the same ground as Wesley, crossing the Ouse, Nene and Bedford rivers and I imagine that in 1747, he would have seen these rivers as pristine new feats of Dutch engineering, now herbage rich and lined with waving poplars. Certainly in February of that year the passage of this route was so grim as to *"...well nigh swallow up both horse and man,"* such was the quantity of fallen snow.

By the mystery of modern propulsion at 10 am I was standing on the eroded pavement outside the London home of John Wesley. There in drizzle under the thunder of city enormity, I stood face to face with a simple abode, almost overshadowed by Wesley's Chapel, the Mother Church of World Methodism. Its façade retains the originality of a Georgian town-house and a wall plaque states the fact that John Wesley (1703-1791) lived there. When I consider his desire and motives for residing in London during his latter years from 1779, compared with a quiet provincial Lincolnshire existence it is easy to comprehend such a move. Even now, when I step out of Epworth Old Rectory, I am still faced with a quaint remoteness whereas this house retains its sense of urgency and dynamism, set as it is within the 'centre of the Georgian world' in terms of social revolution.

As I entered the building I was unprepared for the occurrence that was to follow. The Old Rectory and City Road houses were to be bound together in more ways than I had imagined. It is true that York stone paving welcomes the visitor into both of Wesley's homes, yet my literal journey was about to be enhanced by a matching experience of greater significance.

THE POWERHOUSE OF METHODISM

JOHN WESLEY'S HOUSE, CITY ROAD, LONDON

# The Warm Rooms

My thoughts now go back to the Reverend Samuel Wesley's bedroom in Epworth Old Rectory and its warm welcoming atmosphere, whether created by absorbed daylight of summer's radiance or the sombre blues of a winter's noon; all is equal. We were in London and after jostling with his puzzle of keys, our gentle volunteer guide Stanley Rowland, ushered my wife and me along the narrowest of passages into John Wesley's house.

Images rushed into view as a self-imposed 'museum mentality' took over. Paintings, furniture, artefacts, clothing and books all jumbled together, as I tried to interpret the vision of the place in an urgent desire to assimilate all within. Then it happened. From inside each room the calmness enveloped me; a calm so fixed, permanent and graceful that nothing else was of consequence. The clutter of learning faded, leaving only a pure 'sense of being'. From within The Prayer Room, so small and intimate, yet yielding such spiritual space, I visualised Mr Wesley clarifying his thoughts and gaining strength from his pre-dawn prayers. We gazed upon each room and although the limited light filtered through a rain-filled London sky, the spirit was lifted and nurtured as surely as in Samuel's sunlit Epworth home.

From City Road we ventured along London Wall, The Barbican and towards the grandeur of St Paul's Cathedral. The afternoon Said Eucharist was about to commence and again my soul was uplifted while contemplating receipt of a blessing. It was on the afternoon of the 24th May 1738 that John Wesley had been called to St Paul's after two previous days of *"...continuous sorrow and heaviness in my heart."* In the evening an unwilling visit to a society in Aldersgate Street led to the famous words *"...I felt my heart strangely warmed."* Wesley described this as *"...the change which God works in the heart through faith in Christ."* Eventually during the 25th and 26th May from the very Chancel where I now stood, Wesley stated that he *"...now had peace with God."* My own experience in London had been a memorable one and yet was just one of many to occur during the 'Pictorial Journey'.

THE CHANCEL, ST PAUL'S CATHEDRAL

JOHN WESLEY'S STUDY

# Langham Row - A Marshland Place

It was almost the winter solstice with snow threatening, when I ventured out to find a desolate dwelling known as Langham Row, in the county of Lincolnshire. Both the local historians, William Leary and Betty Kirkham detail this marshland habitation as a significant location, concerning one of John Wesley's Lincolnshire supporters, for here was the home of George Robinson and his large family, known as 'a congregation in themselves'. It was on one of his early visits to the area that John Wesley states, *"I was obliged to preach abroad. It blew a storm and we had several showers of rain but no one went away."*

The Robinsons responded by offering shelter for worship in the form of their granary, encouraging villagers from the surrounding district to join their 'family congregation'. George Robinson who had become a Methodist in 1763, met John Wesley in 1775 and had his own octagonal chapel built on the farm. It was enlarged twice in eighteen years and although no longer standing, served Methodists for more than a century. 'Honest George Robinson' as he was called by Wesley, preached for 43 years and became the first circuit steward. He died in 1813, leaving significant debts that many suggest were due to his commitment to Methodism.

My route from Epworth took me across the Lincolnshire Wolds, a blue-grey stratified landscape, etched upon by skeletal winter boughs and the rich burnt umber of newly ploughed fields. This undulating journey led through the market town of Horncastle via Alford towards the marsh village of Mumby, passing thatched cottages upon which a low liquid sun cast its reflected light, making them glow like tinted alabaster. I saw small pastures and rich winter sward, interspersed by reed fringed dykes, extended to the distant sea bank, over which blew a strengthening icy wind, beckoning further snow flurries to join their fellows in the pantile furrows. Following the main drain out of Mumby, the muddy track ended at a small cluster of buildings. This is Langham Row, now one house cared for by Irene and Herbert Paul, residents for almost sixty years. A kindly man, with a ruddy complexion and the stocky build typical of that locality, Herbert is proud of his heritage and John Wesley's association with the farm.

As I scrutinised the primitive initials *I R 1767*, painted over the door, I could only marvel at the commitment and passion for the gospel that existed within these people. George Robinson had obviously little self regard when giving freely of his limited resources for the benefit of the early Lincolnshire Methodists. As I gazed upon the crumbling remnants of the granary, it was easy to imagine the sound of an enthusiastic chorus as the Robinsons gave praise to the Lord as one exultant voice. Now the day was almost spent with shadows lengthening and distant crows labouring across the chill winter sky, I retraced my steps as the figure of Herbert Paul disappeared into the desolate dwelling known as Langham Row.

FENLAND REED, LANGHAM ROW

# Newbiggin, The Oldest of The Old

The Reverend Richard Hunter seemed to know instinctively who I was as we almost walked into each other beside the Methodist Church in Barnard Castle on the morning of 15th January 2002. Within minutes we were taking tea with local historian Mary Lowe; 'two scones later' my next pilgrimage began. As in many locations, Methodism was established in Teesdale before John Wesley arrived, indeed William Darney who had great influence in Calderdale, preached there in 1747. Wesley's experience in 1752, when addressing the assembled throng for the first time in Barnard Castle, included the famous statement, *"...not a drop fell on me"* due to the fact that a fire engine was brought out to dowse down the fire of Wesley's words! The 'roaring lions' of this town were *"...quiet as lambs"* by Wesley's second visit in 1761! On Tuesday 9th June of that year, he stood in Newbiggin for the first time and would have most likely seen the newly opened chapel of 1760, yet we do not know where he preached on that day.

As I arrived in Newbiggin the visual impact of this dale created a feeling of inferiority brought about by the awesome scale of the landscape before me. Towering heavenward were the great fells, called by Wesley, *"...these horrid mountains"* (he referred to many upland areas as horrid)! Although the village is a placid array of whitewashed farmsteads, the turbulent beck roars through it and on the very summit of the adjacent hilltop stands an even more exposed dwelling. So often on this journey have I been in awe of the 'spirit of a place'. This was no exception. Stepping into the sandstone chapel, still claimed as 'the oldest in continual use', I was again reminded of the warmth of fellowship by my hosts. Within the chapel those great mountains could still be clearly seen through the timber-clad windows and one could sense a reverent and peaceful atmosphere. "Here is the Spirit of Newbiggin," said Richard Hunter. Mary Lowe replied, "Yes, a lot of faithful service and prayer has happened here." We left each other with a feeling of mutual joy. They were filled with a sense of pride and commitment typical of Wesley's people and I was grateful for the moving experience and hospitality.

WESLEY'S PULPIT

NEWBIGGIN, FROM FELLOWSHIP FARM

# The Eight Walls of Yarm

Two spiralling crosses, russet against a pale morning sky reminded me of spiritual references in 'The Windhover' by the poet Gerard Manley Hopkins.

To Christ our Lord
I caught this morning morning's minion, king-
dom of daylight's dauphin, dapple-dawn-drawn Falcon, in his riding...

They were displaying red kites and I was on the road to Yarm in the north-east of England, the date Monday 18th February 2002. My route took me below the towering Hambleton Hills, down into the valley of the river Tees and immediately into a most charming county town; its broad street and cobbled alleys resplendent in their Queen Anne, Georgian and Regency façades. In the centre stood the Manor Court House, carrying a frightening reminder of the flood height of 1771, in the form of an ominous black line. In the distance could be heard the rhythmic thud of a pile drive, busily engaged in shoring up the west bank against more modern insurgences. Indeed, the river Tees was in a post flood state, indicated by all manner of flotsam strewn high upon the dying bank-side alders. How different it looked compared with those youthful boulder-strewn cascades seen in the high dales at Newbiggin, some weeks earlier.

It was on this western bank of the river Tees that I found Wesley's 'favourite chapel', sitting amidst low angular morning shadows cast upon its octagonal form. Here on 24th April 1764 John Wesley states, *"I preached about noon at Potto and in the evening in the new house at Yarm, by far the most elegant in England."* He continues by describing the large congregation attending at five in the morning as being *"...just ripe for the exhortation."* The building had first been used at Christmas in the previous year, opened by Peter Jaco, a local Methodist preacher. It is known that John Wesley greatly influenced the design of The Society House at Yarm, as stated in his correspondence with George Merryweather the local leader of the Methodists during that time. Although up to fourteen octagonal chapels were instigated by Wesley, the building in Yarm by location alone, is worthy of favour. However, it is on entering the building, now somewhat altered since the eighteenth century, that one is struck by Wesley's other statement, *"It is better for the voice and on many accounts more commodious than any other."* When speaking to David Vonberg the present minister, he also viewed the interior with enthusiasm, referring to the tiered, intimate gallery as ideal for the man among his people, designed to reflect the 'theology of the time'. I later viewed the chapel from across the river Tees and was reminded of a violent history that surrounded the formation of many Society meeting places. Was it true that the Nonconformists had been hounded off the main road on to this site by the Anglicans? Did John Wesley actually say about the chapel design, *"There are no corners for the Devil to hide in?"* It was then I felt the first warmth of a springtime noon sun and saw sudden, wayward wind blown movements, across an otherwise placid panorama of water. These sudden surges mirrored the chapel's turbulent past, standing proudly above the river, defying those who originally forced this building to be in such a precarious location. I departed after studying the central roof boss whilst reflecting upon the way in which eight radiating lines are used by the society of this chapel as a source of inspiration, reinforcing their mission to "Love, Live and Share Jesus Christ in their community and beyond."

ACROSS THE TEES. YARM OCTAGONAL CHAPEL

# A Mob -'Like the Roaring of the Sea'

On Friday 21st February 2002, I stood on High Bullen. As a chill north-easterly gale roared up the slope, I stayed just long enough to survey the vast urban space known as the district of Wolverhampton and Shrewsbury. John Wesley preached at this location from a 'horse block', yet little did he know what the future would bring, after his first visit to Wednesbury in January 1743.

Social and economic changes were also occurring in the region at this time. A rich and accessible seam of coal was found at Wednesbury, resulting in immediate industrialisation. Problems associated with poor housing, inadequate sanitation and harsh working conditions prevailed. Hardened blacksmiths, colliers, nailers and forgemen were encouraged by Charles Wesley to join an informal Bible Study group in 1742. This led to a request for John Wesley to found a Methodist Society in the area. Early good relationships between the Methodists and the Vicar of Wednesbury, Edward Egginton soon deteriorated, fuelled by Robert Williams, a local Methodist preacher who dubbed the clergy as 'dicers, carders and dumb dogs'. Although John Wesley called this an "...*inexcusable folly*" the situation was soon out of control with Egginton's call to "Drive these fellows out of the country," being heeded by many in the working populace.

The first outbreak of violence against the Methodists occurred in Walsall and Darlaston. It is here that Justice Persehouse was asked to read the Riot Act in order to protect Methodists, only to wave his hat around and give a comical 'Huzza', the hunting cry of the times. With this legal indifference, the malevolent mob received carte blanche. On 20th October 1743 Wesley arrived in Wednesbury and climbed High Bullen where I stood today. He was soon subjected to the wrath of the Walsall mob while trying to address them. The call for "Knock his brains out" was followed by "Nay, but we will hear him first." Eventually rescued by William Haslewood, the Mayor of Walsall and George Clifton a local prize fighter, Wesley ended the day being delivered "...*safe to Wednesbury, having lost only one flap of my waistcoat and a little skin from one of my hands.*" Riots in the area continued without cessation until February 1744 and included the ruin of every Methodist home in Wednesbury. It wasn't until May 3rd 1745 that Wesley stated, " ...*and has stilled the madness of the people.*"

The one Methodist dwelling that did survive the turmoil is the beautiful childhood cottage of Bishop Francis Asbury. Apprenticed at thirteen years old as a smith at Forge Mill, Francis Asbury became an accredited preacher by the age of twenty one. Five years later during the Bristol Conference in 1771, he found himself being called by John Wesley to travel to the Americas. There he joined The Irish Palatines who had already formed Methodist Societies in New York and Maryland. On questioning his own reasoning for this upheaval to his life, his journal records, "I am going to live to God, and to bring others so to do." Francis Asbury spent forty five years of his ministry travelling over a quarter of a million miles across the untamed west. On his arrival in America there were ten Methodist Ministers. When he died in 1816 there were over six hundred, such was the influence of the man from the Midlands of England. I painted this remnant of strife-ridden times as a tribute to the hardy souls of Wednesbury and Francis Asbury, the product of John Wesley's desire.

A SURVIVOR OF TURMOIL. FRANCIS ASBURY'S HOUSE

# Bristol, Staging Post for the South West

At noon on Palm Sunday 2002, standing on rough hewn cobbles among the ever present murmur of urban life, I was looking at the preachers' stable and entrance to The New Room, John Wesley's Chapel in the Horsefair, Bristol. Little did I know that my hosts for the visit Audrey and David Bainbridge, had invited the organist Harvey French from nearby Horfield Methodist Church, to play the eighteenth century organ, the sound of which pleasantly filled every niche. 'And can it be that I should gain' the well known hymn by Charles Wesley was immediately recognisable, particularly when played upon this chamber instrument built by John Snetzler in 1761. Although John Wesley stated *"Let no organ be placed anywhere till proposed in Conference,"* (and indeed this was acquired in 1930 for the New Room restoration), the rich timbre of each note resonating against fine Georgian panels and the pulpit steps of deepest sienna, created an ambiance that surely must have been enjoyed by those who came here before me. I eventually sat in silence within this wonderful meeting place, the oldest Methodist building in the world and noted a row of pillars illuminated by dappled light, creating subtle, warm tones of pink upon grey stone. The original eighteenth century features; a double pulpit and Italianate lantern windows are still intact, as are the individual preachers' rooms now housing important artefacts that relate to prominent early Methodists. It was here that John Wesley not only initiated his local society meetings but also ran a school for children of the poor and distributed free medicines to their families.

It is widely known that the Wesley brothers spent more time in Bristol than anywhere else in the British Isles, hence the New Room became Wesley's first Conference chapel in 1745 and site of his last Conference in 1790.

The first field preaching was instigated in Bristol by George Whitefield, who introduced John Wesley to the practice on 31st March 1739. Up to that point Wesley states that he had been *"...so tenacious of every point relating to decency and order that I should have thought the saving of souls almost a sin if it had not been done on a church."* However, by April 2nd 1739 he *"...submitted to be more vile"* and spoke to an estimated outdoor congregation of three thousand people in the Bristol brickfields. By May 12th of that year, the first stone of the New Room was laid, *"...with the voice of praise and thanksgiving."*

Of the eighteen Conferences held in Bristol, it is felt that none made a greater impact upon World Methodism than those of 1771 and 1777, during which Francis Asbury and the Reverend Dr. Thomas Coke reinforced their allegiance and 'cast their lot' with John Wesley himself. These individuals devoted their lives to the American ministry, indeed Francis Asbury never returned to England while Dr. Coke became General Superintendent for America in 1784.

My visit over, I left this unique site to the sound of good wishes offered by the people who 'make the place', glad in the knowledge that the work of John, Charles and their early followers still lives on in the heart of Bristol.

INTERIOR, NEW ROOM BRISTOL

# The View from Above

In the year 1771, John Wesley climbed up a hill and found *"...huge rocks, strangely suspended one upon the other."* He was referring to Carn Brea, an area of upland heath located to the south west of Redruth, Cornwall. From this point there is a spectacular panoramic view. To the west lies the Hayle Estuary and St. Ives, to the north the rocky Cornish coastline where it meets the Atlantic Ocean. When surveying the southern vista, there are still at least twenty smelting chimneys in view, a constant reminder of the tin mining heritage and source of human resources for John Wesley. The huge granite boulders of Wesley's time are still in place, perched precariously, some like the partial section of a spine, tossed or stacked as if by the hand of Thor himself.

I sat among the great sleeping giants on the morning of 25th March 2002. The air was still, a shimmering heat having been created by the morning sun in a clear blue sky; absolute silence punctuated only by the distant clamour of jackdaws as they spiralled around the mine chimneys. This lofty vantage point reminded me of an illustration in my junior Bible depicting the temptations of Jesus in the wilderness. There below life was going on; the farmers, fishermen and industrialists of modern Cornwall, engaged in their centuries old daily toil. One was aware of the nearness to God when brought to such a high point as this. How would John Wesley have felt, particularly when viewing those many poor souls toiling below? The southern panorama of mines remains very much the same to this day as it did in 1771, only now they are as silent as the air about the huge natural sculptures of Carn Brea.

TIN MINE, REDRUTH, CORNWALL

CARN BREA, A VANTAGE POINT

# The Tin Miners' Legacy

Between 1762 and 1789, John Wesley preached eighteen times from an amphitheatre formed by the disused mine known as Gwennap Pit, in the hamlet of Busveal near Redruth, Cornwall. His first use of the ground occurred on 5th September 1762 when a high wind forced him to vacate his usual place at Gwennap. Described by John Wesley as *"...a round, green hollow, gently shelving down, about fifty feet,"* in which his hearers were *"...commodiously placed, row upon row,"* it became immediately apparent that the Pit formed a natural auditorium and was to be of great value to his preaching. The Journal spanning those two decades shows how the Pit realised its potential with congregations numbering many thousands. Indeed Wesley's own account of August 22nd 1773 states, *"There must be above two and thirty thousand people...Perhaps the first time that a man of seventy had been heard by thirty thousand persons at once!"* Whether inflated numbers or not, we are certain that many thousands attended and indeed villages would have been without many of their inhabitants when Mr Wesley was at the Pit.

These images came to mind while I sat on the outer edge of the Pit, above Boundary Cottage, on the afternoon of March 25th 2002. The exterior banks were adorned with wood anemones, primroses and newly emerging crocosmia. Spring birdsong abounded, the blackbird's flute and a robin's distinct trill both heralding the joy of the moment. At the base of the Pit a family sat on a blanket, engaged in pleasant conversation whilst preparing a picnic. The young man spoke softly about 'John's Place' as his tousle haired daughter scampered around the amphitheatre enjoying her new found playground. From within one could appreciate the intimate nature of this original preaching place, with ears turned to and eyes focussed on the preacher from all around. Although remodelled in 1806, the present feature still evokes a splendidly powerful emotion, particularly when another distant tin mine chimney can be glimpsed, reminding us again of the working population whose lives were changed on this very spot by the words of John Wesley. Elleanne, as I discovered she was called, had now begun to re-enact 'The Three Little Pigs' story using Mr Wesley's granite pillars as 'The House of Stone'. How joyful to see this stage through the eyes of a child, a perfect analogy mirroring the bygone innocence of the many converts who had thronged here. My final encounter was with Daisy and Ernie Blackmore, guardians of Gwennap Pit and Busveal Chapel. What a joy to hear their account of eighty years in the vicinity and witness the pride in their ability to be of service to the multitudes who have visited over the years. Ernie spoke of the hundreds of miles of grass cutting and pointed out that it is about a mile to the bottom of the Pit if you walk each terrace to the depths and back!

**THE GATEPOST PULPIT, GWENNAP**

GWENNAP PIT

# The Hepping Stock of St Buryan

Sir Humphrey Davey, inventor of the miners' safety lamp hailed from Cornwall and according to family tradition, was blessed as a small child by John Wesley after a church service. The preaching sites of John Wesley in Penzance are difficult to identify, being referred to in his journals as *"in a meadow"* or *"on a cliff."* We do know that in 1747 he preached at Western Green on the coast towards Newlyn. He became in imminent danger from an anti-Methodist mob and was rescued by Philip Kelynack, known as 'Old Bunger' and Peter Jaco, both from Newlyn. How often do we read of locals 'coming to the rescue' of Mr Wesley? Certainly, this occurred many times.

From Penzance I journeyed in search of the 'hepping stock' of St Buryan. This village lies to the south-west of Penzance en route to Lands End. The Anglican Church stands at its centre and next to the gate is the feature known as the hepping stock. This is a set of very large stone steps, built apparently in bygone days for a very large squire to mount an even larger horse! From documentary evidence, it seems that John Wesley got on the wrong side of the Reverend Robert Corker, the curate of this parish. It appears that in 1747 Robert Corker told an untruth to his whole congregation by saying, "Now Wesley has sent down for a hundred pounds and it must be raised directly, nay it is true." Wesley wrote to the curate putting matters straight, yet as always, bad feelings abounded and on 7th September 1766 the Journal records, *"At 8 I preached in Mousehole... Thence I went to Buryan Church and,...preached near the churchyard... I saw a gentleman before me, shaking his whip and vehemently striving to say something. But he was abundantly too warm to say anything intelligibly. So after walking awhile to and fro, he wisely took horse and rode away."* The hepping stock became Wesley's vantage point, although it wasn't until the death of Robert Corker that he could preach here without duress. On my return to Gwithian, our base for the Cornish experience, I stopped at Marazion. As the tide was low I retraced the steps of John Wesley across the causeway to St Michael's Mount. In 1745 Wesley climbed The Mount while waiting for a case against one of his preachers to be heard by the local justices, whom they described as an "able-bodied man without lawful calling or sufficient maintenance." Wesley was accompanied on this day by the vicar of St Gennys, the Reverend George Thompson who himself became known as 'the first Cornish Methodist'. It is recorded that in later years on being informed that Parson Thompson was dying, Wesley immediately rode from Camelford to St Gennys where he gave Thompson his final communion. Thus the high esteem in which John Wesley held dear one of his travelling companions is again apparent.

ST. MICHAEL'S MOUNT

THE SQUIRE'S MOUNTING BLOCK

# A Tale of Ursula Triggs

It is not often that one is able to speak with a direct descendant of those who were original members of a Methodist Society. On 28th March 2002 I was able to do just that and must say that it was a humbling experience. The story takes place on the western coast of The Lizard peninsula, Cornwall overlooking Mullion Cove and the jagged headland of Men-te-heul. I was in search of a link between the Mullion Methodist Society of the late 1760s and the wonderful Angrouse Cottage still standing quietly today near Mullion village, amidst a working Cornish farm. Good fortune had led me to Mr William Hendy, presently living in the 'new' Angrouse Farm where he would recall the history of this ancient house.

The first indication we have of Methodism reaching the area was at the hands of William Hitchens from Gwennap, described as 'one of Wesley's itinerant preachers from 1745-1758.' He was met with violent opposition and suffered such tribulation that he 'relinquished his object.' However it was at that time that Ursula Triggs became noticeable for her many well known feats of endurance, perseverance and above all, persuasion. Ursula was the daughter of the parson in Mullion, the Reverend John Wills. She had married Thomas Triggs, a well-to-do farmer in 1748 and they lived in Angrouse, the location that would soon form a central position in our unravelling tale. Ursula had been impressed by William Hitchens, apparently rescuing him and other preachers, from mob persecution at Bennets Well, near Mullion. Described as 'a robust woman with a commanding personality and a dominant person with some authority', it is known that Ursula rode on horseback to St John's near Helston, a round trip of fourteen miles, to hear John Wesley preach during 1753 or 1755. She then regularly made the same journey to attend bible classes after 1760 and eventually became leader of the Angrouse Society. A room was made available in her house and prayer meetings were held on Sunday afternoons. It was also at her request that John Wesley asked William Hitchens to make another attempt at preaching, such was the mutual understanding between the two. It is said that she 'found peace with God' after hearing Mr Wesley and on 7th September 1762 received his blessing at Angrouse House itself. The occasion was a notable one on two accounts. First, John Wesley writes about the Mullion community in his journal by saying, *"How tender are the hearts of this people!"* This was possibly followed by the baptism of Ursula's youngest son, John Triggs by Wesley himself. (As an Anglican parson he was entitled to do so). The Mullion Society referred to John Wesley as "That great messenger of Christ" and marked his preaching place with a small boulder which bears the inscription *S T 1762*. This has now been set into a stone wall by the field opposite the old house.

Angrouse House, formerly known as 'Grouse', is recorded in 1317 to have been called 'Crous', meaning a wayside Catholic shrine. Gazing upon it I was filled with a sense of humble spiritual pride for my memory is now filled with the imagery of Bill Hendy, sitting beside his Methodist Long Service Certificate which states 'Preacher of the Year, 1952'. His aged fist punched the air with a fervour of passionate zeal as he stated quite clearly, "My paternal grandmother was the daughter of John Shephard. He was the youngest son of Elizabeth Triggs, Ursula's daughter." There were tears of elation and pride from us all, in the knowledge that Bill's story had continued to be told on that joyful spring day above the sea of Mullion Cove.

ANGROUSE, MULLION

# Jack's House, Trewint

I left Cornwall on 29th March 2002, by virtually the same route that John Wesley and his three companions had taken on first entering the county in 1743. East of Bodmin we crossed the moor, an open expanse of bleached grasses and scattered gorse, shimmering in the heat haze of the continuing hot, spring spell. Our journey followed an eighteenth century coach road, now the busy A30, artery to the south-west. John Wesley, William Shepherd, John Nelson and John Downes had originally made their way from Launceston on 29th August 1743. Whilst the former pair travelled on towards Bodmin, even losing their way and eventually regaining it by the sound of bells, Nelson and Downes only reached Trewint by which time they were in need of sustenance. (They actually had one horse, and rode by taking turns.) They came upon 'the house with the stone porch' and sought refreshments from Elizabeth Isbell, the wife of Digory, a local stonemason. She welcomed the travellers and so impressed John Nelson that he returned to stay some weeks later, preaching at 7 am the next morning to a large congregation. Digory Isbell's reaction to the original visit by Nelson and Downes was recorded by Francis Truscott, an itinerant preacher, in his conversation with one of the Isbell's daughters. It appears that on Digory's return, Elizabeth detailed the strangers' ways and manner of preaching and his comment was, "I have read somewhere in the Bible, how some have entertained angels unawares."

The Isbell conversion was by now complete and they were determined to be of service to any of John Wesley's preachers who passed Trewint, being so strategically situated for their travels across the peninsula. It is to this hospitality that John Wesley came, staying on at least six occasions.

THE HEARTH, WESLEY'S COTTAGE

The Isbells even added two new rooms to the house, including 'The Prophet's Chamber' specifically designed for use by the preachers. It is said that this came about after they read II Kings 4:8-11, with reference to the visit of Elisha and the Shunamite woman who said "Behold now, I perceive that this is a holy man of God, which passeth by us continually. Let us make a little chamber..." Digory saw this as a direct divine command, resulting not only in the extension to his house but also because it became a focus for worship. John Wesley continued his visits, sometimes standing in the porch of the house. A small society was also formed in the locality and revival services have taken place there in later years.

I was welcomed that day by Joyce Pooley, the present caretaker of Trewint Cottage, just as John Nelson had been in 1743, by the Isbells. At just over five feet in height, Joyce entered the cottage with the same ease as Wesley would have done and made it easy to imagine the preacher standing in the ancient porch. He had summed up the progress of Methodism in Cornwall on 15th July by the words, *"Indeed I never remember so great an awakening in Cornwall, wrought in so short a time, among young and old, rich and poor, from Trewint quite to the seaside."* Those sentiments had been reinforced in Cornwall as I remembered the kind words of Bill Hendy, the warmth of Daisy Blackmore and the joy of Elleanne as she scampered with her Christian family in the Pit at Gwennap. I left Jack's House, Trewint so named with reference to little Jacky's escape from the Epworth fire, in joyful anticipation of where my next place of pilgrimage might be. On passing the cottage garden, I read a sign that says 'To all pilgrims, this garden offers rest, beauty and peace'. So be it, with thanks to those hardy travellers of 1743.

**TREWINT COTTAGE**

# A Journey to the South East

Even the newly opened apple blossom in the kitchen garden had an air of melancholy as I emerged at 5.45 am on Sunday 21st April 2002. Not quite knowing if I had in fact woken up; my thoughts turned to Mr. Wesley and his habitual pre-dawn practices wherever he found himself. My journey then began with an almost immediate recuperation occurring as adrenalin took over. Three motorways later I found myself compiling colour notes in the most charming of God's Acres. In front of me towered the church of St Mary in Bexley, on the south-east fringes of London. Known as a 'candle snuffer' the upper tower exterior comprises of oak shingles while the main structure is of flint composition.

Members of the Anglican congregation were most welcoming and spoke of the Wesleyan movement in Bexley during the vicariate of the Reverend Henry Piers, 1737-1770. Henry Piers accepted both John and Charles Wesley to such an extent that there was no requirement for a Methodist Church to be built in Bexley. Henry Piers was also instrumental in the all important first introduction to the Reverend Vincent Perronet, the vicar of Shoreham, who was soon to be an influential figure with regard to future matters of Methodism. The Wesley brothers first came into contact with Bexley due to their mutual friend, Mr Charles Delamotte of nearby Blendon Hall. Delamotte actually accompanied the Wesleys to Georgia in 1735 and also knew the Reverend George Whitefield. Through this notable association, both George Whitefield and Charles Wesley were welcomed to preach in Bexley church during 1737. Parish records of 1742 also indicate the baptism of Anne Wood, Sarah Barnes and Edward Clark by Charles Wesley that year. As each baptism was by immersion, it is assumed that the nearby river played its part.

THE OLD YEW, SHOREHAM

ST. MARY'S CHURCH, BEXLEY

# Into the Darent Valley

Like John Wesley, my next logical route radiated out from London towards the south-east, a softened landscape of hanging woodlands and chalk escarpments so typical of the Kentish North Downs. Tracing the river Darent, racing along its valley as a true babbling brook complete with kingfisher and wagtail, I encountered for the first time the 'suntrap' village of Shoreham. My time in the village was to be a joyous one, experiencing first hand the intimate locations frequented by our missionary traveller.

The Wesley brothers first came to Shoreham after Wesley's introduction on 14th August 1744 to the Reverend Vincent Perronet, by the Reverend Henry Piers, vicar of Bexley. This relationship between Perronet and the Wesleys was described as one of 'deep sympathy and understanding which was to develop and endure for the rest of his long life'. Indeed, Perronet was Vicar of Shoreham from 1728 to 1785. His empathy with the Methodist movement and in particular his support for lay preaching, earned him the greatest of accolades from John Wesley himself. Wesley called him *"...that venerable saint"* and prayed that he *"...may follow him in holiness."*

In true Methodist style, all was not easy from the outset, for when Charles Wesley preached on the first occasion in the church during 1744, the congregation acted like *"...wild beasts, roaring and storming, blaspheming, ringing the bells and turning the church into a bear garden."* On this occasion Vincent Perronet hung over Charles to take the blows. When John Wesley preached, 'the beasts' turned out of The George public house and stoned the preacher to such an extent that Perronet's coach was sent to the church in order to deliver him safely a mere sixty yards to the vicarage.

I was privileged to meet Susan and Frank Hinks of The Old Vicarage, who were glad to tell stories in the original rooms where so much of significance had taken place. On entering the vicarage, set in spacious gardens bedecked with fresh spring foliage of the purest viridian, I was immediately drawn towards the principal parlour in which John Wesley would regularly preach on Sunday evenings. Adjacent was the kitchen favoured by Damaris, the 'bold, masculine minded' eldest daughter of Vincent, who became leader of the Methodist Society in Shoreham. In 1776, Wesley wrote of Damaris, *"A chief instrument of this glorious work is Miss Perronet, a burning and shining light."* The kitchen, also used by Damaris as a school room, bears a curious resemblance to Susanna's kitchen in Epworth Old Rectory. Many original features remain including the shutters, fireplace and bread oven. One intriguing remnant of early use shown to me was a fine example of eighteenth century graffiti. (*P. Perronet 1735* had been etched upon an open shutter.) Our conversation soon revolved around the possibility of a bored scholar seeking distraction by his illicit labours! Such was the importance of Perronet's interaction with the Wesley brothers that they called him the 'Archbishop of Methodism'. It is well known that he became their chief source of arbitration, either when settling quarrels, resolving personal questions of marriage, or giving advice regarding ministerial policy.

My day ended as it had begun, yet with added nostalgia, for on leaving the sign for Biggin Hill my journey north took me past Duxford and The Imperial War Museum. Over the motorway roared both Spitfire and Hurricane in close formation, a fitting reminder of where in England I had been.

THE OLD VICARAGE, SHOREHAM

# Romance and the Robin

We were more than half way to central Wales when we decided to enjoy our evening picnic along that rutted Shropshire lane. Thin wisps of dandelion danced by while above sang a yellow bunting, its repetitive song of 'bread and cheese' so typical of a tangled hedge in May. Blossom of fruit orchards and thorns glowed like incandescent beacons as we hurried to reach our destination before nightfall. On the morning of Saturday 11th May 2002 we travelled from Crossgates, south-east of Rhayader to Builth Wells and Garth, location of another significant episode in the lives of the Wesleys. It was here in 1749 that John Wesley officiated at the wedding of his brother Charles to Sarah Gwynne, daughter of Squire Marmaduke Gwynne. Interesting cross references occurred at this stage in our journey for into the frame stepped yet again the inimitable Vincent Perronet of Shoreham. Apparently, apart from his 'want of fortune' Sarah's mother had not entirely objected to Charles Wesley as a suitor for her daughter. Having not impressed his future mother-in-law with his £50 legacy and pending publication of hymns, he returned to London with a heavy heart. In true spirit of friendship and support, Perronet wrote to Mrs Gwynne extolling the virtues of Mr Wesley and putting a publisher's value on the hymns in excess of £2,500. This obviously had the desired effect as Mrs Gwynne gave immediate consent by letter to Shoreham.

THE WEDDING ROUTE, GARTH

So it was that at 8 o'clock on Saturday 8th April 1749, the wedding party left Garth House to walk the short distance to Llanlleonfel Church. I eventually reached this vantage point after meeting Betty and Eric Hamblett who reside at Tyn-y-llan, 'house by the church'. I can only describe these sincere people as both charming and generous with their time, tea and lunch! Their purposefully designed and thoughtfully planted gardens are some of the most delightful we have encountered, perched as they were on the hillside and seeming to be an integral part of the church environs and surrounding natural landscape. Looking towards Garth House across the wedding route I considered John Wesley's state of mind on the day of the marriage, due to his description of it as *"...a solemn day, such as became the dignity of a Christian marriage."* They would have forded the river Dulas, followed by a laboured ascent of the rushy hillside upon which I now stood. John Wesley must have surely felt a sense of pending loss by virtue of the fact that his brother and companion was about to enter wedlock.

Distant Garth House sat partially screened by protective conifers and as the splashes of colour below Epynt-Myndd changed momentarily from light to dark, I visualised the circumstances that resulted in the 'robin and the storm' tale now so convincingly engrained in local lore. This story, had it been true, could have added vitality to an already wonderful vision. Unfortunately, the subsequent hymn was written in 1740, prior to Charles Wesley's first visit to Garth,

> "Hide me O my Saviour hide,
> Till the storm of life be past."

It would have been comforting to think that these lines, part of the famous hymn 'Jesu, Lover of my Soul' could have been composed after Charles Wesley saw an unfortunate robin attempting to shelter in the parlour of Garth House during a severe storm. My thoughts returned to the present, the colour composition being limited to a chosen viewpoint, unfortunately omitting many adjacent sensory pleasures; a nearby hillside smothered in bluebells, the liquid song of a garden warbler and the plaintive bleating of new-born lambs. After leaving the Hambletts in their lofty paradise, we continued our journey by following the river Wye from Builth Wells in an attempt to retrace John Wesley's crossing of the Black Mountains towards Devauden, his first preaching place in Wales.

THE RIVER WYE, BUILTH WELLS

## 'The Star' below Devauden Hill

The river Wye tumbled on, close to our south-easterly route out of Builth Wells and it appeared that the shimmering beeches had become clothed overnight in their pristine cloaks of green. From Talgarth, almost unawares, we were thrust into the valley of the river Usk and from the east the awe-inspiring Black Mountains began to dominate the landscape. I could not help noticing the few remaining eighteenth century farmsteads still clinging to those hillsides and found it difficult to comprehend how the intrepid Wesley brothers would have made their way from Bristol.

As colour notes were compiled below Mynydd Llsiau, I studied each plane between foreground and distance. My focus took me upward across a delicate treescape, past miniature stone structures, stands of gorse and finally to the bracken covered slopes themselves. In Lincolnshire, where landscape is full of sky, surely in Wales the sky is full of land! On reaching Abergavenny, the countryside softened as sweeping valleys, stands of conifers and arable cropping edged into the pasture lands. We eventually came upon Devauden, nestling among a cluster of heavily wooded hills, overlooking our former route, now a mere 'pencil mark' upon the horizon. It is here that, on the afternoon of 15th October 1739, John Wesley first preached in Wales. As with other locations, he had been 'invited', in this case by a number of supporters including Griffith Jones and Howell Harris. Over three hundred people attended that first gathering, comprising of wood colliers (charcoal burners) and labourers, forming a responsive congregation for Wesley's sermon on *"Christ our wisdom, righteousness, sanctification and redemption."* By good fortune, my research took me to Veddw House, home of the garden writer Anne Wareham, whom my wife Jacqui happened upon by the village green. Copies of old documents in Anne's collection led me to search for 'Nexey', the house where John Wesley stayed during his visit to Devauden. Unfortunately nothing remains of the original house so we took Wesley's original westward route in search of 'The Star' where he lodged; describing it as *"A good though small inn."* Conveniently placed inland of the Severn landing point at Chepstow, the inn's location allowed me to trace Wesley's earliest route into Wales. As I stood outside 'The Star' and sketched the snaking road as it meandered out of sight, my thoughts turned to those people of Wales whom Wesley had found to be *"Ripe for the Gospel and earnestly desirous of being instructed in it."* From our experience, it appears that earnest Methodists are still active in Wales, in some instances forming joint pastorates for the good of often remote rural communities.

LANDSCAPE, THE BLACK MOUNTAINS

# Newcastle, Third Point of the Triangle

In my experience the people of Newcastle are honest, welcoming, forthright souls. This was certainly the case when John Wesley became familiar with them, as outlined in his journal quote of 4th June 1759. *"Certainly, if I did not believe there is another world, I should spend all my summers here, as I know no place in Great Britain comparable to it for pleasantness."* By direct contrast, Wesley's earliest encounter with the populous of 1742 had been represented by the words *"I was surprised; so much drunkenness, cursing and swearing (even from the mouths of little children) do I never remember to have seen and heard before in so small a compass of time."*

So it was that I ventured out with an expectant air under a mackerel sky on 18th June 2002, hoping to meet the Reverend Terence Hurst, minister in charge of Brunswick Methodist Church, at the very heart of Newcastle itself. On meeting Terry, we set off in search of The Keelman's Hospital, an imposing building situated above the old quays of the river Tyne and adjacent to the bank known as 'Lousy Hill', scene of Wesley's 5 o'clock sermon on Sunday 30th May 1742. It had been my desire to paint an image that conveyed information about the grandeur of Newcastle, yet on entering the hospital courtyard, one of Charles Wesley's favoured open air preaching places, I became subject to a feeling of claustrophobia. I then noticed the lofty presence of the nearby building known as Garth Head and fuelled by a cocktail of opportunism and good fortune gained access to the building. There below stood the Keelman's Hospital, its courtyard enclosed by the great city, itself framed by the Tyne Bridge, a symbol of strength and unity. It was here that John Wesley was described by a resident as "a bonny little man, with such a canny nice face." Historical evidence recalls that he was also protected, nursed and loved by particular ladies of the town. An early engraving depicts the 'muckle fishwife' Mrs Bailes with protective arms around the preacher as she screams, "If ony yen o'ye lifts another hand to touch ma canny man, a'll floor ye directly." She continued by running along with Wesley's horse down to Sandgate, uttering "Noo touch the little man if yer dare!" John Wesley spent the princely sum of £70 to secure land upon which to found The Orphan House, a purpose built structure that would act as meeting room, chapel, library, school and hostel. Although never to house orphans, it became the third significant site alongside The Foundery in London and New Room in Bristol to complete the Methodist triangle. Wesley's only real tribulation in Newcastle came as a result of his relationship with Grace Murray, a lady of 'masculine independence and feminine grace' who had become committed to his work by acting as manager of the Orphan House. She looked after the needs of travelling preachers, nursed the sick (including John Wesley himself) and was also entrusted with pastoral and spiritual duties. Grace accompanied Wesley to Ireland in 1748 and became very close, only to be parted by the intervention of brother Charles, who not only suggested to Grace that her marriage to Wesley would be a 'disaster for Methodism' but also arranged for a speedy wedding ceremony to take place between her and John Bennet, a local travelling preacher on 3rd October 1749, while John Wesley was in Whitehaven.

As I left Newcastle to the echoing cry of a paper seller beneath the monument of Charles, Earl Grey, another advocate of civil and religious liberty, I heard the words of Wesley in his eighty seventh year as he left Newcastle for the last time, *"A lovely place and people."*

THE KEELMAN'S HOSPITAL, NEWCASTLE

# Methodists in Calderdale

I was fortunate to discover the name John Nelson during my exploration of Cornwall, only to find out that he had actually originated from Birstall in Yorkshire and like Digory Isbell of Trewint, was a stonemason by trade. Could it be that their profession had initiated a simple bond between the two men? Nelson had heard Wesley preach at Moorfields in London during 1739 and was changed from "...a wandering bird, cast out of the nest" to one who's soul was "...filled with consolation, through hope that God for Christ's sake would save me." Nelson returned to Birstall and founded the first Methodist Society there in 1741. John Wesley followed, possibly in 1742 when he came to Smith House, Lightcliffe. He certainly arrived on 22nd August 1748 in support of the Noncomformists who had roots in Calderdale since the sixteenth century Protestant Reformation. It is on the 25th August that his Journal accounts from Roughlee indicate a direct initiation into the Methodist movement for the formidable Reverend William Grimshaw, vicar of Haworth and stalwart supporter of the Wesleys by being pushed to the ground. The mob then *"...loaded them both with dirt and mire of every kind."* Well known for his 'unrestrainedly evangelical ministry', Grimshaw had initially tried to turn his parishioners away from John Nelson's preaching at Keighley in 1744 saying, "Wherever the Methodists go they turn everything upside down." The influence of William Darney, a roving Scottish preacher who settled into Methodist discipline by 1747 finally changed the vicar's attitude. Just as Vincent Perronet of Shoreham had done, Grimshaw's firm and supportive friendship with Wesley grew. He used his robust behaviour and speech to whip up congregations across the region. My favourite expletive uttered by this forthright fellow to an unsympathetic audience was, "If you will go to hell, you shall at any rate go with the sound of the gospel in your ears!"

Grimshaw became superintendent and evolved the early circuit, which became known as 'The Great Howarth Round'. It is by way of this circular route that I travelled, visiting Halifax, Heptonstall, Bingley and Greengates, north-east of Bradford. At Heptonstall I found yet another unique octagonal building, the chapel of 1764, opened just three months after Yarm in Teesdale. After stumbling and tumbling along the narrow slabbed street I descended on to a hillside terrace overlooking a yawning valley encased by endless moorland. Described as "...an unspoilt church in dramatic medieval and Jacobean setting" this meeting house is a direct result of William Darney's early work and formation of the Society in Heptonstall. John Wesley took over the Society in the late 1740s returning several times during the next decade to preach to immense and enthusiastic crowds. On 6th July 1764 he preached in the shell of the new building, dedicating it at the same time.

I was to find myself alone on the upper balcony of this fascinating building on 17th July 2002. Three sounds could be heard; the distant chatter of visiting school children, a jaunty melody from a practising soprano and finally, the drone of a solitary fly as it tried to find its way to light and air on this day of sticky humidity. I eventually emerged from the chapel on to the dappled, fern covered terrace likening my own spiritual circumstances to that of the incarcerated fly, who's struggle for basic freedom was a poignant reminder of my own hazy vision. I was gratified by the thought that I am not the first or last mortal to be phased by such uncertainty.

HEPTONSTALL, CHAPEL ON THE TERRACE

# Yorkshire Grit

Having trekked by upland fields of drying hay, I came upon the austere gritstone walls that surround Mount Zion Methodist Church below Ovenden Moor on the edge of Halifax, West Yorkshire. Captivated by its rugged form and ability to stand unaided for many years, I was reminded of the vigorous Methodist endeavour within the region that has also stood the test of time. On meeting Irene Cunliffe, the local heritage secretary, I was welcomed by an enthusiastic dialogue and tour of the unique building, including the preacher's cottage in which her local minister had recently fallen through the floor! Complete refurbishment however, has ensured that the building has become a useful future resource.

The first Methodists in north Halifax began to meet in a cottage along nearby Bradshaw Row during 1748, initiated by the fervour of James Riley who had heard both John Wesley and William Grimshaw preach in the locality. On 22nd April 1774 John Wesley visited 'Bradshaw House' as it became known and described it as *"...standing alone in a dreary waste."* By now however, a strong following had become established and the people flocked from all quarters. It is also recorded that there was once an intriguing hand etched inscription found on one of the diamond shaped panes of the cottage window. It said 'Time how short - eternity how long. CW.' Does this suggest that 'brother Charles' may have been in residence during those early pioneering days? In May 1790, less than a year before his death, John Wesley preached to great crowds and rested that night in private quarters at the cottage, yet another 'prophet's chamber' like the inner sanctum of Trewint.

Leaving Bradshaw and a group of distant gyrating banshees known as a wind farm, I continued on 'The Round' to Bingley in search of Myrtle House, known by Wesley as *"..a little paradise."* This imposing dwelling is now Bingley Town Hall.

My final destination within the vast Leeds and Bradford conurbation was Woodhouse Grove School, brought directly into Methodist control by a question at the Conference of 1781. When asked if a school for the sons of Methodist ministers could be erected in Yorkshire, similar in style to Kingswood to the south, Wesley replied *"Probably we may. Let our brethren think of a place and a master and send me word."* When Woodhouse Grove estate was finally acquired for £4,575 this was the largest single financial outlay made by the Connexion up to that time. The new school was to be called The Wesleyan Academy at Woodhouse Grove, although its present title seems to have remained in constant use throughout history. The school eventually opened in 1812 with two masters and nine boys, all or whom were indeed sons of Wesleyan ministers. The eighteenth century estate parkland now supports fine sporting grounds for current pupils, all of whom are fortunate to attend such an academy of excellence.

MOUNT ZION, BRADFIELD

# The Manors of Oxfordshire

On the 31st July 2002 the sky was as dull as a scholar's slate. Soaked, half cut wheat stood forlornly across Lincolnshire as roads became rivers on that sunless dreary day. By mid morning I had entered Oxfordshire, glad to be standing before Finstock Manor, once family home to generations of the Bolton family particularly with reference to the wonderful Anne or Nancy, *"My Dear Sister"* as John Wesley would address her. My personal discovery of the Finstock connection with early Methodism came about by the most remarkable of coincidences. During breakfast at 'The Shearwater Guesthouse' on St Mary's, Isles of Scilly some weeks earlier, I had spoken to a fellow guest about a beautiful patchwork quilt made in Finstock and featured in the illustration of Epworth Old Rectory. The response by the Reverend Peter Hutchings, a retired minister, was immediate and animated as his grandfather had married a member of the Bolton family, one of the last generations to live at The Manor. He had also been evacuated there in 1940 and remembers being shown the exact location where John Wesley had preached beneath a cabinet, in the unaltered kitchen.

Nancy Bolton originated from Blandford Park, Witney; she probably met Wesley in 1764 after which they frequently and purposefully corresponded. Wesley obviously fell in love with Nancy's words and deeds for she became the dependable helper at Witney. Her letters were to become a constant source of spiritual enlightenment and joy. To Nancy, John Wesley was a treasured friend, guide and councillor whose written word from afar became a poor substitute for his sublime countenance. In a letter of 29th February 1772 he wrote, *"I rejoice over others, but over you above all."* In a letter to a fellow preacher he compared Nancy to other ladies of the circuit with the words, *"You have not such a flower in all your gardens."* Over the years their correspondence rather intensified, Wesley addressing himself as *"Your Affectionate Brother"* adding pleasantries such as *"Thou perfect pattern of womanhood."* Fuelled by this encouragement, Nancy Bolton remained faithful to Wesley, marrying some time after his death in 1791, continuing resolutely with the mission to which she had been granted such entitlement.

Moving on from Finstock the rain was now both vertical and violent making field sketches a rather tedious occupation. However, on negotiating a bend in the river Thames I reached the exquisite village of Stanton Harcourt, once home to the Reverend John Gambold, incumbent from 1735 to 1743 and very close friend of John Wesley during his student days in Oxford. It was he who had so often seen Wesley come from his time of prayer with "serenity that was next to shining." By the parish church of St Michael I found 'Ivy Cottages', now known as 'Wesley's Cottage' due to the fact that John, Charles and their sister Kezia had sometimes stayed there. It was here that Wesley brought the Moravian, Peter Böhler, for an important meeting with John Gambold, who later became a Moravian Bishop. Eventually, my studies were hastily completed with the help of Rita Stockhill, an enthusiastic local Methodist and permission granted by the Honourable Mrs Gascoiyne, Lady of Harcourt Manor. From here I headed towards Oxford in search of academic facts associated with Wesley's early years.

FINSTOCK MANOR

# Methodical Living

The intimate Oxfordshire landscape, occasionally interspersed by distant undulating vistas, is home to many wonderful watercourses, the most notable being the rivers Thames, Evenlode and Windrush. Throughout history rivers such as these became arteries from which much of England's trade and transport evolved. The eighteenth century saw a sustainable rural economy become influenced by technology; water power attracting the attention of millers and bargees. It is into this changing environment that John Wesley, the newly ordained deacon of 19th September 1725 would make small excursions, taking services in local village churches. It has been widely accepted that his first sermon had been delivered at South Lye (Leigh) near Witney in 1727. However, recent diary research by the historian Professor Richard Hietzenrater and others, suggests that Wesley's first sermon was preached at Fleet Marston on 3rd October 1725 to be repeated in 1727 at South Lye.

Wesley became a Fellow of Lincoln College on 17th March 1726. Despite serious study he did however seek to develop a social life and became friendly with several families in the Cotswolds, particularly in the villages of Stanton, Broadway and Buckland. Diaries reveal that he also entered into intimate correspondence with a pair of 'pious and cultural ladies' whom he 'christened' 'Selima' and 'Aspasia'. Wesley's early days in Oxford created a situation in which a distinct formula for his later practice became apparent, particularly in relation to his use of time, and structured methodical manner of living. This became clearly expressed by the role Wesley played in a small study group set up at Christ Church, along with his brother and a mutual friend William Morgan. Initially ridiculed by some fellow students, this group drew membership from various colleges and became dubbed 'Bible Moths', 'Sacramentarians' and eventually 'Methodists'. It wasn't until 1762 that Vincent Perronet called the United Societies the 'Methodist Church'. John Wesley's own dictionary of 1753 clearly stated *"A Methodist is one who lives according to the method laid down in the Bible."* Their own loose title for the group, first used in November 1732, was 'The Holy Club'. This title, although only lasting six months in Wesley's day, has in fact stood the test of theological time.

My exploration of Lincoln College, led me around hallowed quadrangles each displaying an immaculate master's green. The specific college rooms used by Wesley are not clearly defined as he may have used several. I viewed the restored area containing Wesleyan artefacts and particularly enjoyed the portrait of Wesley by J. M. Williams. Completed during 1742 the work cleverly portrays a hidden sense of activity and sustained labour, described by the Reverend R. Green as having the eyes of "one with a calm, steady, penetrating gaze with which he arrested the leaders of the riotous mobs." For my own painting, I decided upon a viewpoint to include the 'possible' rooms used by Wesley including his place of worship, the college chapel, as a prominent feature. My tour of Oxfordshire had been a stimulating one, for not only had I retraced the steps of Wesley but also sourced new personal accounts of Methodist heritage alongside existing academic data. The July rain continued for days and as a consequence many homes throughout Europe were flooded. Despite struggling with the elements, my enthusiasm for this fascinating man had certainly not been dampened.

LINCOLN COLLEGE, OXFORD

# Over the Firths to the Totum Kirkie

We began our final journey on Saturday 25th October 2002, heading further north than on all previous occasions. On passing Yarm and Newcastle I had a distinct feeling that even Wesley's thirst for adventure would have been adequately quenched by this tour. Yet tour he did, visiting Scotland on no less that twenty-two occasions between 24th April 1751 and 2nd June 1790. His visits were centred upon Edinburgh and Glasgow, with a tendency to include east coast settlements, occasionally reaching the south-west towards Dumfries and Galloway. Wesley's most impressive journey however, although viewed by some as irresponsible due to inclement weather, must have been that of 25th April 1770. Ignoring advice given to him at Dalwhinnie, his party ventured into the highlands. They finally completed a circular route by 10th May, which included Inverness, Nairn, Aberdeen and Dundee.

As dusk descended, we had scarcely reached the border villages below Coldstream, passing squat stone cottages, timeless and strong, yet conspicuous and melancholy due to their austere remoteness. It is well documented that our preacher's time in Edinburgh created both approval and friction, culminating in his arrest on 4th June 1774. (He referred to it as one of the dirtiest towns that he had ever seen). We mingled with international visitors whilst searching for the High School Yard off Infirmary Street, scene of several sermons by Wesley. My dismay at not being able to locate a suitable viewpoint, fuelled a more urgent desire to stride briskly to the Royal Mile in search of another early Methodist site known as Bailie Fyfe's Close. Of the numerous 'closes' on the High Street, many having associations with prominent eighteenth and nineteenth century Scots, this time-worn threshold appealed to me enormously. It led into an enclosed courtyard, from which access to a tenement house could be gained. It was unlike any society meeting place that I had ever encountered. During 1761, Wesley preached in this intimate space, sheltered from the elements and such was its immediate charm that I had no choice but to include it in A Pictorial Journey.

ARBROATH TOTUM KIRKIE

Reluctantly leaving Edinburgh, we crossed the great straths of Forth and Tay before following Wesley's east coast route to Arbroath. It was from here that the local minister, the Reverend Mary Patterson had given specific instructions in order to find the last remaining Scottish octagon. We were to seek Fleming's the butcher's shop which was conveniently situated opposite the chapel. I made enquiries from a pleasant lady in the street, (who by sheer coincidence happened to be a member of the Methodist congregation) and her astonishment was followed by, "Surely the English are not coming up here for Fleming's famous steak pies!" Wesley first came to Arbroath during his highland tour on Tuesday 8th May 1770, returning bi-annually over the years. Although Methodism never took root in Scotland as it did in England, some committed societies had already formed prior to Wesley's visit, assisted by the work of Thomas Cherry from Swaledale, who by 1768 had created a framework for further development in the area. Arbroath chapel was actually opened by Wesley in 1772 and became known as the Totum Kirkie, the name being derived from an eight-sided spinning toy. I was assisted in the collection of data for my chapel viewpoint by senior steward David Nicholl which included balancing on a very high wall! I imagine the reader can guess what our supper comprised of on reaching the far shores of Cullen. Yes indeed, it was a very filling and rather famous Fleming's steak pie!

**BAILIE FYFE'S CLOSE**

# Charm by the Edge of the Sea

The town of Banff, viewed in pale afternoon light as it nestled neatly below a headland overlooking the river Deveron, was exactly as I had visualised it. Everything had a pristine quality, busy and filled with vitality yet without the grime and trappings of urban culture. Our early arrival meant that a little exploring could take place prior to meeting Alison Borrowman, our local Methodist contact. I wandered down old Fife Street on to Battery Green, the very place where John Wesley had preached on 20th May 1776. As with many of these coastal settlements one can sometimes chance upon the architectural remnants of an earlier community. In this case, the cottages had housed fishermen and their families, the very core of a working population so sought after by the early preachers.

John Wesley described Banff as, *"One of the neatest and most elegant towns that I have seen in Scotland. It is pleasantly situated on the side of a hill, sloping from the sea, though close to it, so that it is sufficiently sheltered from the sharpest winds..."* I had certainly been drawn to it by this statement, fully endorsing the observations and sentiments of Wesley. The progress made by the early society in Banff was not without difficulties, although sheer remoteness and lack of good roads in Wesley's time did little to help matters. John Wesley even received criticism from society members William and Isabel McPherson, after his 1776 visit due to the fact that they felt neglected. Their strength of feeling was reiterated in a letter to the preacher Robert Dall, "...he supped at Lord Banff's and the next night at Admiral Gordon's Lady's house, with a great number of great ones; and at their request he preached in the English chapel to an elegant and crowded congregation." It is assumed by some, that this reference to the English chapel, created an opportunity for those who wished to label Wesley as a Jacobite sympathiser. Nothing came of this however and the Methodist profile in Scotland continued to rise, if not in volume, then certainly in influence.

We travelled westwards from Banff to the sweeping bay of Cullen to find another unique jumble of cottages discreetly tucked away behind the sea wall. The community of Seatown was to be our base for a few days, courtesy of the Reverend Ray Cummins, local minister and salmon fishing enthusiast! With recent snows glistening upon the Cairngorm mountains and a bitter chill in the air, we were glad indeed of such a cosy bothy. Our final exploration in this forgotten corner took us to Fochabers, reached by Wesley on 30th April 1770 when he waited there at the inn. On seeing the river Spey previously he had stated, *"We rode thence to the Spey, the most rapid river next the Rhine that I ever saw."* I chose to sit on the old tollhouse bridge, contemplating this magnificent surge of foaming water as it roared beneath my feet, creating spirals of liquid sepia as if drawn by a fine quill. Gazing down-river, the Spey danced its way through curls of deepest indigo until lost from view as an ice-blue ribbon upon a landscape of bronzed beeches. Lasting memories of Wesley's journey to the far north are firmly etched upon my mind like frosty cirrus trails spreading so delicately across the morning sky. Beneath them, thin wisps of grey geese were also making their long journey to the south.

OLD FIFE STREET, BANFF

# Home at Last

Epworth Old Rectory was described by W. Le Cato Edwards as 'A delightful and satisfying Queen Anne building' and was home to the Wesleys for thirty-nine eventful years. A document of 1607 indicates that the original parsonage consisted of 'five baies, built all of timber and plaister; and covered all with straw thache.' It also appears that my ancestors were neighbours at that time as the statement concludes '...and of John Maw, - sonne of Thomas, - his tenement and a croft on the north.' The Maws continued as farmers and millers into the late nineteenth century, my great-grandfather John Henry Maw being named in Kelly's Directory of 1889.

Standing on Greengate, gazing across the Rectory croft, I recollected many occasions when I had been thrilled and truly heartened by the Methodist presence in Epworth. Realising that my unruly clambering over the Rectory rubble had occurred in 1956 when the building was in its most serious state of disrepair, it dawned upon me that I was only five years old at the time, so obviously I must have been led astray by older children! I visualised summer fayres in the croft, garden parties on the lawns and more recently, the resident flock of sheep cared for by the Reverend Gordon Gatward, our charismatic minister of the early nineties. My thoughts soon turned to the many wardens, volunteer guides, caretakers and gardeners who have worked tirelessly for the Rectory, entertaining visitors so expertly over the years.

Finally, I considered the meaning of pilgrimage and what purpose lie behind A Pictorial Journey if indeed any did. Remembering H. L. Gee's sheer joy in the closing pages of his quaint little book, 'Easter at Epworth' and his prayers for the 'gallant Methodist garrison', it became clear that my journey too had been one of spiritual exploration. Living at the epicentre of World Methodism for so long, I had made incorrect assumptions about the wider world without knowing it. Are Methodist people strong, united and passionate about their heritage? Do they hold precious their links with John Wesley through physical locations and the knowledge that his word has been spoken there? From the windswept granite of Mullion to the homely orchards of Kent; across the high mountains of Wales to the verdant pastures of Ireland, consistency prevails. Yes, there is a united Methodism and just as our preachers faced the challenges of the eighteenth century, so the people of the new millennium face theirs.

THE RECTORY CROFT

EPWORTH OLD RECTORY

# Acknowledgements

John Hurst sincerely thanks the following people for their local knowledge, hospitality, friendship and genuine desire to assist in the completion of his 'pictorial journey'.

Cornwall
- Colin Short
- Dr Chris Blake
- Howard Curnow
- John C. Probert
- Mr Tony Langford
- Brian Ede, Redruth
- Katherine J. Smith, St. Just
- William, Elsie, Adrian Hendy and family, Angrouse Farm, Mullion
- Christopher Burgoyne, Mullion
- Roger Green, Launceston
- Joyce Pooley, Trewint Cottage
- Frank Brice, Liskeard
- Daisy and Ernie Blackmore, Gwennap Pit
- Mr & Mrs J. Gollop, Gwithian

Bristol New Room
- Mark Topping
- David Bainbridge
- Rachael Newton

John Wesley's House and Chapel, 49 City Road, London
- The Reverend Dr Lesley Griffiths M.A.
- Ms Noorah Al-Gailani, M.A., curator
- Stanley Rowland, volunteer guide

Ireland
- Ivor Owens, Birr, Co. Offally
- John Purdey, Adare, Co. Limerick
- Angela Mell
- Bernadette Foley
- Kenneth Todd, Co. Cork
- Dudley Leviston Cooney, Dublin
- Tom and Mary Alexander, Gloster House, Birr, Co. Offally
- Brian Ruttle, Ballingrane, Co. Limerick
- M. O'Donnell, Adare Golf Club

South East
- Harvey Richardson
- Susan and Frank Hinks, The Old Vicarage, Shoreham, Kent
- Barbara and Peter Knight, Shoreham, Kent
- Valerie Bowlzer, Bexley, Kent
- Gladys Atfield, Bexley, Kent

North East
- Graham Carter, Darlington
- Les Hann, Weardale Circuit
- David Vonberg, Stockton Circuit
- David Bucktrout, Whitby
- Dr Stuart Burgess, York and Hull District
- Terence Hurst, Brunswick Methodist Church, Newcastle

Teesdale
- Richard Hunter, Barnard Castle
- Mary Lowe, Barnard Castle
- Mr & Mrs Makepeace, Fellowship Farm, Newbiggin

Lincolnshire
- Betty Kirkham, Hogsthorpe
- David Robinson
- Herbert and Irene Paul, Langham Row
- Jim English, Library Archivist, Epworth Old Rectory
- Hamer Savage
- Dr E Huckett
- Mr & Mrs. A. Milson, Epworth Old Rectory
- Mr & Mrs L. Churchill
- Mr R. Fish and the Governors of St. Martin's C. of E. School
- Mr G. Trinder
- Mr Max Gray
- Mr David Keal
- David Rushton
- Paul Waterfield

Wales
- William Morrey
- Barbara Bircumshaw
- Michael and Carol Langstaff, Llandegley, Powys
- Mr Eric & Betty Hamblett, Llanlleonfel
- Peter Curry
- Anne Wareham, Devauden
- William Griffith

Midlands
- Donald Cross, Wednesbury

North West
- Gordon Terry
- Irene Cunliffe, Heritage Secretary, Mount Zion Methodist Church
- Woodhouse Grove School

Oxfordshire
- Dr Timothy S.A. Macquiban
- Mrs Rita Stockhill, Stanton Harcourt
- Roger Faulkner, Witney
- The Hon. Charles and Amanda Cayzer, Finstock Manor
- Roy Townsend, Finstock
- Mr & Mrs P. Hutchings
- Professor Paul Langford, The Rector, Lincoln College, Oxford
- With special thanks for permission to reproduce the William's portrait, courtesy of Lincoln College, Oxford

Scotland
- Dr Niall Sinclair and Dr Rosemary Webb
- Mrs Margaret Batty, Edinburgh
- Mary Patterson and Mr David Nicholl, Arbroath
- Alison Borrowman, Banff

Sincere thanks to the Reverend and Mrs Ray Cummins for the loan of the wee house in Cullen.

With special thanks to the Reverend Dr Nigel Collinson for the foreword, Mrs Jacqui Hurst for type setting and navigation, Victor and Judy Shirley for such a good idea. With additional thanks to Mr & Mrs A. Milson, Epworth Old Rectory for their tolerance and understanding.

With very special thanks to Peter Forsaith, Wesley & Methodist Studies Centre, Westminster Institute of Education, Oxford Brookes University, for his careful scrutiny of the text!

# Bibliography

The Wesleys and West Yorkshire—John Hargreaves M.A.

Mount Zion, Ogden, 1773-1973—John Bradley

Thunderclaps from Heaven—John Munsey Turner

Methodist Beginnings in the North East—John C. Bowmer

The Methodist Church Today-In Newcastle—R. J. Doidge

A History of Newcastle-upon-Tyne—S. Middlebrook

John Wesley and Oxford—Dr V.H.H. Green

Moments in Time at Stanton Harcourt

My Dear Sister—Maldwyn Edwards

The Methodist Church, 1999 Directory—Methodist Publishing House

The Journal of John Wesley-STL Edition, Percy Livingstone-Parker

The Works of John Wesley, edited by W. Reginald Ward and Richard P. Heitzenrater

Primitive Physic, J. Wesley edited by William Paynter

John Wesley, Foundery Pamphlets—Cyril J. Davey

The Wesley Family and Their Epworth Home—Maldwyn Edwards

Epworth, the Home of the Wesleys—W. Le Cato-Edwards

The Wesley Trail—Cornish Tourist Board

John Wesley in Devon—Michael Wickes, M.A.

The Keepers of Absalom's Island—Tom Nestor

The Irish Palatines—Dudley Levistone Cooney

A Guide to Irish Country Houses—Mark Bence-Jones

The Houses of Ireland—Brian de Breffny, Rosemary Ffolliott

Limerick, The Rich Land—Sean Spellissy, John O'Brien

Irish Place Names—Deirdre Flanagan and Laurence Flanagan

Lincolnshire Methodism—William Leary

The Wesleys in Cornwall—John Pearce

In the Steps of the Wesleys—F.C. Gill

The Early Methodist People of Lincolnshire—William Leary

The Brackenbury Memorial Lecture, 1985—Betty Kirkham

Newbiggin Chapel, Its Place in History—Mary Lowes, Lorne Tallentire

Yarm Methodist Chapel, A Brief History—Arthur George

The Bitter Sacred Cup, The Wednesbury Riots, 1743-1744—J. L. Waddy

Bishop Francis Asbury, Prophet of the Long Road—E. Benson-Perkins

New Room—Maldwyn Edwards

Francis Asbury—Peter W. Gentry

The Historical Tablets of the New Room, Bristol

Methodism in Mullion—Ivor Thomas

St Mary's Church, Bexley—Miss K.M. Roome

A Particular Glory—Katherine Moore

Shoreham, A Village in Kent—Malcolm White, Joy Saynor

Fedw Villages—Raymond Howell

A History of Monmouthshire—Sir Joseph Bradney

A Hymn Lovers' Companion—C.P. Hancock

Arbroath Methodism—George W. Davis

Wesley in Scotland—George W. Davis

Exploring Scotland with Wesley—The Synod of the Methodist Church in Scotland

Easter at Epworth—H. L. Gee, Epworth Press, 1944

# Useful Addresses

The Methodist Church Conference Office
Methodist Church House
25 Marylebone Road
London NW1 5JR

The Methodist Publishing House
4 John Wesley Road
Werrington, Peterborough
PE4 62P

The Methodist Church Archives and Research Centre
The John Rylands University Library of Manchester
150 Deansgate
Manchester M3 3EH

The Convener
Wesley & Methodist Studies Centre
Oxford Brookes University
Harcourt Hill
Oxford OX2 9AT

Englesea Brook Methodist Chapel and Museum of Primitive Methodism
Englesea Brook
Crewe  Cheshire CW2 5QW

Wesley's Chapel, House and Museum
49 City Road
London EC1Y 1AU

The Old Rectory
Rectory Street
Epworth
North Lincolnshire

# Index

| | | | | | |
|---|---|---|---|---|---|
| Aberdeen | 16,66 | Bodmin | 46 | Cummins, Ray | 68 |
| Abergavenny | 54 | Böhler, Peter | 62 | Cunliffe, Irene | 60 |
| Adare | 20,22 | Bolton sisters | 10 | Dall, Robert | 68 |
| Aldersgate Street | 26 | Bolton, Nancy | 62 | Dalwhinnie | 66 |
| Alexander, Tom | 18 | Borrowman, Alison | 68 | Darent river | 50 |
| America | 34 | Boundary Cottage | 40 | Darent Valley | 50 |
| Anglicans | 32,44,48 | Brackenbury, Robert Carr | 16 | Darlaston | 34 |
| Angrouse | 44 | Bradford | 58,60 | Darney, William | 30,58 |
| Angrouse Cottage | 44 | Bradshaw | 60 | Davey, Sir Humphrey | 42 |
| Angrouse House | 44 | Bradshaw House | 60 | deBreffny & Ffolliot | 18 |
| Arbroath | 16,67 | Bradshaw Row | 60 | Deel river | 20 |
| Asbury, Francis | 34,36 | Bristol | 34,36,54,56 | Delamotte, Mr Charles | 48 |
| Atlantic | 22,38 | Broadway | 64 | Devauden | 53,54 |
| Bag Enderby, Great Elm of | 14,22 | Brunswick Methodist Church | 56 | Deveron river | 68 |
| Bailes, Mrs, muckle fishwife | 56 | Buckland | 64 | Downes, John | 46 |
| Bailie Fyfe's Close | 66 | Builth Wells | 52,53,54 | Dublin | 18,22 |
| Bainbridge, David & Audrey | 36 | Busveal | 40 | Dulas river | 53 |
| Ballingrane | 22 | Busveal Chapel | 40 | Dumfries & Galloway | 66 |
| Banff | 68 | Cairngorm mountains | 68 | Dundee | 66 |
| Banff, Lord | 68 | Calderdale | 58 | Dunraven Estate | 20 |
| Barbican, The | 26 | Camelford | 42 | Duxford | 50 |
| Barnard Castle | 30 | Camoge river | 20 | Earl Grey, Charles | 56 |
| Battery Green | 68 | Carn Brea | 38 | Edinburgh | 66,67 |
| Bedford river | 24 | Chapel, John Wesley's | 36 | Egginton | 34 |
| Bennet, John | 56 | Chepstow | 54 | Embury, Philip | 22 |
| Bennets Well | 44 | Cherry, Thomas | 66 | England | 32,34,50,64,67 |
| Bexley | 48,50 | Christ Church | 64 | English Chapel | 68 |
| Bible Moths | 64 | City Road, London | 24,26 | Epworth | 10,12,22-28,47,50,70 |
| Biggin Hill | 50 | Clifton, George | 34 | Epynt-Mynda | 53 |
| Bingley | 58,60 | Coke, Dr Thomas | 36 | Evenlode river | 64 |
| Bingley Town Hall | 60 | Coldstream | 66 | Fife Street | 68 |
| Birch, 'Lamorna' | 42 | Conference, Methodist | 34,36,60 | Finstock | 10,62 |
| Birr | 18 | Cooney, Dudley | 22 | Finstock Manor | 62 |
| Birstall | 58 | Corker, Robert | 42 | Firths | 66 |
| Black Mountains | 53,54 | Cornwall | 38-47,56,58 | Fleet Marston | 64 |
| Blackmore, Ernie & Daisy | 40,47 | Cotswolds, The | 64 | Fleming's Butchers | 67 |
| Blandford Park, Witney | 62 | Crossgates | 52 | Fochabers | 68 |
| Blendon Hall | 48 | Cullen | 67,68 | Forbes, Stanhope | 42 |

| | | | | | |
|---|---|---|---|---|---|
| Forth | 67 | Holy Club, The | 64 | Maigue river | 20 |
| Foundery, The | 56 | Holyhead | 7 | Manor Court House | 32 |
| Franciscan ruin | 20 | Hopkins, Gerard Manley | 32 | Marazion | 42 |
| French, Harvey | 36 | Horfield Methodist Church | 36 | Maryland | 34 |
| Gambold, John | 62 | Horncastle | 28 | Maw, John | 70 |
| Garth | 52 | Horsefair, Bristol | 36 | Maw, John Henry | 70 |
| Garth Head, Newcastle | 56 | Hunter, Richard | 30 | Maw, Thomas | 70 |
| Garth House | 53 | Hurst, Terence | 56 | McPherson, William & Isabel | 68 |
| Gascoiyne, Hon. Mrs | 62 | Hutchings, Peter | 62 | Men-te-heul | 44 |
| Gatward, Gordon | 70 | Infirmary Street | 66 | Merryweather, George | 32 |
| Gee, H. L. | 70 | Inverness | 66 | Methodism | 12,22,28,30,47,48 |
| Georgia | 48 | Ireland | 12,18,22,56,70 | | 56,62,67 |
| Georgian | 24,32,36 | Isbell, Digory | 46,47,58 | Methodist Society | 22,34,44,50,58 |
| Glasderry More | 18 | Isbell, Elizabeth | 46 | Methodists | 12,16,20,28-36,54-57 |
| Glasgow | 66 | Ivy Cottages | 62 | Moorfields | 58 |
| Gloster House | 18,20 | Jack's House | 46,47 | Moravians | 62 |
| Gordon, Admiral | 68 | Jaco, Peter | 32,42 | Morgan, William | 64 |
| Great Howarth Round, The | 58 | Jacobean | 58 | Mount Zion Methodist Church | 60 |
| Green, R. | 64 | Jacobites | 68 | Mousehole | 42 |
| Greengates | 58 | Jones, Griffith | 54 | Mullion | 44,70 |
| Grimshaw, William | 58,60 | Keelman's Hospital, The | 56 | Mumby | 28 |
| Gwennap Pit | 40,44,47 | Keightley | 58 | Murray, Grace | 56 |
| Gwithian | 42 | Kelynack, Philip | 42 | Mynydd Llsiau | 54 |
| Gwynne, Mrs | 52 | Kentish North Downs | 50 | Myrtle House | 60 |
| Gwynne, Sarah | 52 | Kezia | 62 | Nairn | 66 |
| Gwynne, Squire Marmaduke | 52 | Kingswood | 60 | Nelson, John | 46,47,58 |
| Halifax | 58,60 | Kirkham, Betty | 28 | Nene river | 24 |
| Hambleton Hills | 32 | Lands End | 42 | Nester, Tom | 22 |
| Hamblett, Betty & Eric | 53 | Langham Row | 28 | New Room, The | 36,56 |
| Harcourt Manor | 62 | Launceston | 46 | New York | 22,34 |
| Harris, Howell | 54 | Leary, William | 28 | Newbiggin | 30,32 |
| Haslewood, William | 34 | Leeds | 60 | Newcastle | 56,66 |
| Haworth | 58 | Limerick | 18,20,22 | Newlyn School of Artists | 42 |
| Hayle Estuary | 38 | Lincoln College, Oxford | 64 | Nexey | 54 |
| Heck, Barbara | 22 | Lincolnshire | 16,24,28,54 | Nicholl, David | 67 |
| Hendy, Mr William | 44,47 | Lincolnshire Wolds | 14,28 | Nonconformists | 32,58 |
| Heptonstall | 58 | Lizard peninsula | 44 | Old Bunger | 42 |
| Hietzenrater, Prof. Richard | 64 | Llanlleonfel Church | 53 | Old Rectory, The | 10,24,26,50,62,70 |
| High Bullen | 34 | London | 24,26,48,52,56,58 | Orphan House, The | 56 |
| High School Yard | 66 | London Wall | 26 | Ouse river | 24 |
| Hinks, Susan & Frank | 50 | Lousy Hill | 56 | Ovenden Moor | 60 |
| Hitchens, Mr William | 44 | Lowe, Mary | 30 | Owens, Ivor | 7 |

| | | | | | |
|---|---|---|---|---|---|
| Oxford | 62,64 | Shrewsbury | 34 | Wareham, Anne | 54 |
| Oxfordshire | 10,62,64 | Shunamite woman | 47 | Wednesbury | 12,34 |
| Palatines | 12,20,22,34 | Smith House, Lightcliffe | 58 | Wesley, Charles | 34,36,48,50-53, 56,60,62 |
| Patterson, Mary | 67 | Snetzer, John | 36 | | |
| Paul, Herbert & Irene | 28 | Society House, Yarm | 32 | Wesley, John | 10-69,70 |
| Pearce, Sir Edward Lovatt | 18 | South Lye (Leigh) | 64 | Wesley, Samuel | 10,26 |
| Penzance | 42 | Spey river | 68 | Wesley, Susanna | 10,50 |
| Perronet, Damaris | 50 | St. Buryan, Heppingstock of | 42 | Weslyan Academy, The | 60 |
| Perronet, Vincent | 48,50,52,58,64 | St. Gennys | 42 | Wesley's Chapel, Bristol | 36 |
| Persehouse, Justice | 34 | St. Ives | 38 | Wesley's Chapel, London | 24 |
| Piers, Henry | 48,50 | St. John's, Helston | 44 | Wesley's Cottage | 62 |
| Pooley, Joyce | 47 | St. Mary's, Isles of Scilly | 62 | Western Green | 42 |
| Potto | 32 | St. Mary's, Bexley | 48 | Whitehaven | 56 |
| Prayer Room, The | 26 | St. Michael's Church | 62 | Whitefield, George | 36,48 |
| Prophet's Chamber, The | 47 | St. Michael's Mount | 42 | Williams, John | 64 |
| Protestant Reformation | 58 | St. Paul's Cathedral | 26 | Williams, Robert | 34 |
| Purdy, John | 22 | Stanton Harcourt | 62 | Wills, John | 44 |
| Queen Anne | 32,70 | Star, The | 54 | Windrush river | 64 |
| Raithby | 16 | Stockhill, Rita | 62 | Witney | 10,62,64 |
| Rathkeale | 20,22 | Swaledale | 67 | Wolverhampton | 34 |
| Redruth | 12,38,40 | Tay river | 67 | Woodhouse Grove School | 60 |
| Rhayader | 52 | Tees river | 32 | Wye river | 54 |
| Rhine river | 68 | Teesdale | 58 | Yarm | 32,58,66 |
| Riley, James | 60 | Thames river | 62,64 | | |
| Riot Act | 34 | Thompson, George | 42 | | |
| Robin Hood's Bay | 12 | Tolgarth | 54 | | |
| Robinson, George | 28 | Totum Kirkie | 67 | | |
| Roscrea, C. Offaly | 18 | Trent river | 24 | | |
| Roughlea | 58 | Trewint | 46,58,60 | | |
| Rowland, Stanley | 26 | Trewint Cottage | 47 | | |
| Royal Mile | 66 | Triggs, Elizabeth | 44 | | |
| Ruttle, Brian | 22 | Triggs, Thomas | 44 | | |
| Sacramentarians | 64 | Triggs, Ursula | 44 | | |
| Scotland | 66,67,68 | Truscott, Francis | 46 | | |
| Seatown | 68 | Tullamore, Co. Offaly | 7 | | |
| Selima & Aspasia | 64 | Tyne Bridge | 56 | | |
| Severn river | 54 | Tyne river | 56 | | |
| Shannon river | 20,22 | United Societies | 64 | | |
| Shearwater Guesthouse, The | 62 | Usk river | 54 | | |
| Shephard, John | 44 | Vonberg, David | 32 | | |
| Shepherd, William | 46 | Wales | 52,53,54,70 | | |
| Shoreham | 48,50,52,58 | Walsall | 34 | | |

THE RIVER SPEY

JOYCE POOLEY AND THE ARTIST
AT TREWINT